First Governor
First Lady

First Governor First Lady

John & Eliza Routt of Colorado

Joyce B. Lohse

Published by
FILTER PRESS, LLC
P.O. Box 95
Palmer Lake, Colorado 80133
www.filterpressbooks.com

Front cover photograph: Denver Welcome Arch from Union Station,
L.C. McClure, photographer (ca.1906) courtesy of Denver Public Library,
Western History Department, MCC-835.
Back cover photographs:
John Routt portrait courtesy of Colorado Historical Society, F-5202.
Eliza Routt portrait courtesy of Colorado State University.

Library of Congress Cataloging-in-Publication Data

Lohse, Joyce B. (Joyce Burke), 1950–
First governor, first lady : John and Eliza Routt of Colorado / Joyce B. Lohse; foreword by Richard D. Lamm.— 1st edition
p. cm.
Includes bibliographical references (p.) and index.
ISBN 0-86541-063-1 (pbk.)
Routt, John Long, 1826-1907. 2. Routt, Eliza Pickrell, 1839-1907. 3. Governors—Colorado—Biography. 4. Governors' spouses—Colorado—
Biography. 5.
Colorado—Biography. 6. Frontier and pioneer life—Colorado. 7. Colorado—History—1876-1950. I. Title.

F781 .R855 2002
978.8'031'092—dc21
[B]

2001050810

Printed in the United States of America

To Mom

&

Eliza

Contents

Routt Gravestone, Riverside Cemetery, Denver, Colorado.
Photographer: Joyce Lohse (1999).

Acknowledgments

I WISH TO THANK EVERYONE who assisted me along the way and made this book possible. They include: Doris Baker of Filter Press; Colorado Historical Society; Colorado State Archives; Denver Public Library, Western History Department; Fairmount Cemetery Company; Dr. James E. Hansen, Colorado State University historian, and John Buffington, CSU photographic services; Richard and Dottie Lamm, former governor and first lady of Colorado; Thomas J. "Dr. Colorado" Noel, history professor, University of Colorado at Denver; Dr. John Y. Simon, executive director, Ulysses S. Grant Association; and Women Writing the West.

I also thank Ivan Brunk, Nancy Burke, Sandy Coyer, Paul Idleman, Judy Kosanovich and clan, Don Lohse, Charlie Lohse, Jean Lohse, Carol McCloskey, Susan Oakes, Francell Schraeder, and the Routt family descendants for their support and encouragement. I especially appreciate my Pickrell ancestors who connected me to Eliza and John Routt.

Colorado State Capitol, ca. 1900. *Courtesy Denver Public Library, Western History Department*, MCC-289. Photographer: L. C. McClure.

Foreword

MY WIFE, DOTTIE, was asked by Joyce Lohse to write a foreword to this book, but I asked Dottie if I could do it instead. I have always been fascinated by the role of women in various times of history. The historical status of women does not reflect well on my gender, but that is a long story going back to the dawn of time. I graduated from law school in 1961, and there was one woman in my law school class. It never occurred to us that women would want to become lawyers. Today over fifty percent of those enrolled in law school are women.

Women who are ahead of their time have always fascinated me. The courage, intelligence, or guts it took a woman in the nineteenth or early twentieth century to go to medical school, run for office, or participate in any meaningful way in the world of men never fails to intrigue. Modern women stand on the shoulders of giants. Eliza Routt was one of those giants.

Colorado has never had a woman governor. Wyoming has, as have a number of other states. Colorado's time will come; it almost came in 1998, when Gail Schoettler was defeated by only 8,000 votes. Also on the 1998 ballot, running for the U.S. Senate was my wife, Dottie. For thirty-eight years, Dottie has joined me (and lately exceeded me) in interest in and dedication to public policy. When I was running for the legislature in 1966, she walked blocks with me knocking on doors; two years later, she repeated the block-by-block canvas with our first child, Scott, on her back. Dottie took a bus to Selma, Alabama, in 1965 to march with Martin Luther

King. She has traveled to Cairo, Egypt, and Peking, China, fighting for women's rights. I have always recognized that she would have been a better politician than I was. But she arrived on the political scene too early for her own career so she worked tirelessly on mine. I can never repay the debt I owe her.

In the Governor's Mansion we were partners in many things. In addition to having a newspaper column in the *Denver Post* and raising our two children, Dottie always had time to head a task force on some important subject, cover for me in a speech or campaign appearance, take a leadership role in the governor's conference programs for spouses, or host a last-minute dinner. She was wife, political advisor, political partner, and priceless campaign asset.

We were in office 100 years after the Routts. We read their story with great interest and across the years sympathize with many of their victories, problems, stresses, and challenges. We live in vastly different times, but we identify so much with their lives.

It must have been a paradox in restrained Victorian society to have progressive views on social issues such as suffrage, then to act upon them. The 1870s and on must have presented different challenges, but the human side is similar. The working out of a partnership in marriage is hard enough, but doing it in a fishbowl is even harder.

"Women of the West" is a popular subject right now. This book focuses on Eliza Routt for her involvement in social issues, specifically in the suffrage movement. The defining moment of her involvement would have been when she was chosen to be the first woman registered to vote in Colorado. That moment opened the door for women to serve in public office and for her to become the first woman on the State Board of Agriculture and to start the School of Domestic Economy. The goal of a woman senator or governor has not been reached yet, but Eliza Routt pioneered the path and constructed the early bridges.

John and Eliza Routt appeared to work as partners, as did Dottie and I. Eliza set an example for all future wives by showing that it is possible to work as partners to achieve good things in life and for the community, without succumbing to a contest of egos or of the sexes.

This is a story about the birth of Colorado. The Routts did an effective job of ushering the territory into statehood and were important in forming the state's character in those tenuous early days.

What sets the Routts apart is that they exhibited the utmost integrity in their actions and nonpartisan treatment of others in the interest of doing their best for their family, state, and community. How important and rare are these qualities in public life today.

RICHARD D. LAMM
Colorado Governor,
1975–1987

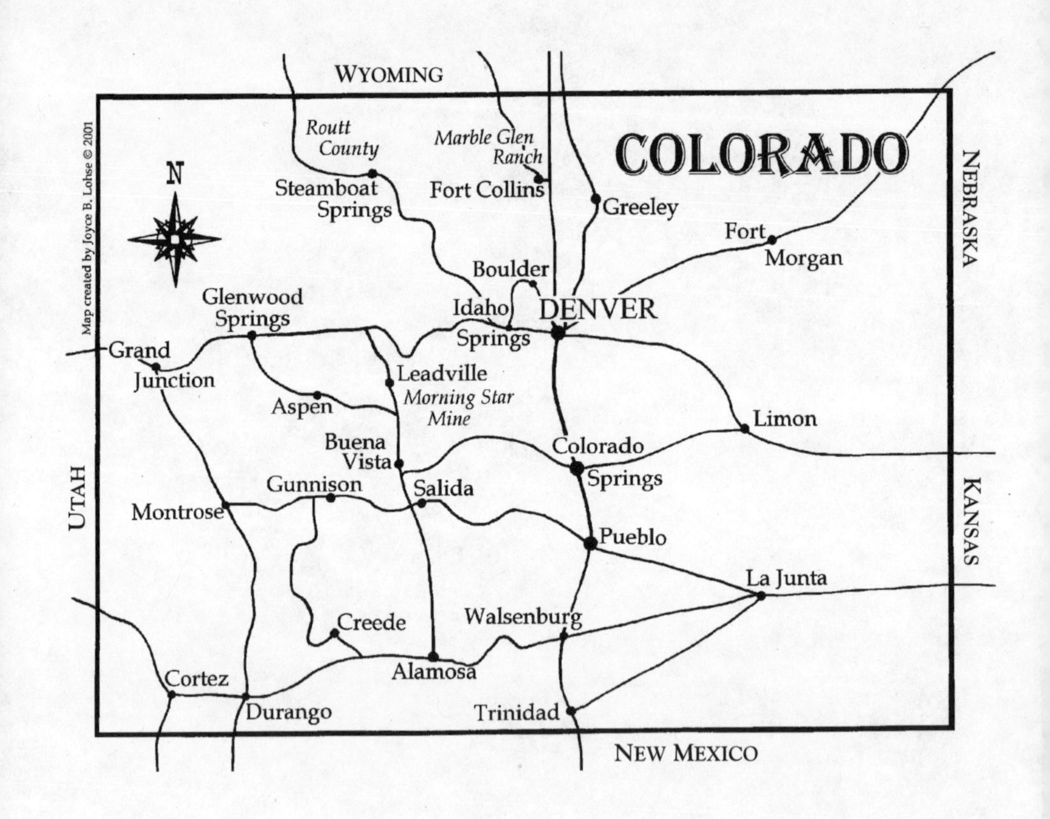
COLORADO
WYOMING
NEBRASKA
KANSAS
NEW MEXICO
UTAH
N
Map created by Joyce B. Lohse © 2001
Routt County
Marble Glen Ranch
Steamboat Springs
Fort Collins
Greeley
Fort Morgan
Boulder
Idaho Springs
DENVER
Glenwood Springs
Grand Junction
Leadville
Morning Star Mine
Aspen
Limon
Buena Vista
Colorado Springs
Gunnison
Salida
Montrose
Pueblo
La Junta
Creede
Walsenburg
Alamosa
Cortez
Durango
Trinidad

In Search of the Routts

JOHN AND ELIZA ROUTT'S story begins where it ended, at Riverside Cemetery in Denver, Colorado. Located north of downtown Denver on the banks of the Platte River, Riverside Cemetery is the final resting place of many Colorado pioneers and historically significant people, and is designated a national historic district.

On one of those mild, sunny days in December that provide a welcome interlude from winter weather, I went to Riverside Cemetery in search of the Routts. Genealogy research had introduced me to Eliza Pickrell Routt (rhymes with "scout"), an ancestral cousin on my mother's side. A short paragraph in a Pickrell family genealogy booklet mentioned that Eliza Pickrell had married Colonel John Routt and listed two of his three terms as governor and also referred to his work toward building the Colorado State Capitol. Routt's title as "present governor of Colorado" appeared in a short line in the 1876 edition of the *History of Early Settlers of Sangamon County, Illinois*, a book about the county in which Eliza's family were pioneers.

Virtually all of my ancestors for the past five generations had settled in Illinois. Consequently, I was thrilled to find that Eliza, who had married Colorado's first governor, had lived in my adopted home state of Colorado. As a journalist, I felt compelled to learn more about the times in which they lived and to share their story.

Considering John Routt's importance as a public figure, I assumed it would be an easy matter to find out more about this interesting couple. I soon learned this was not the case. Along with the Routts themselves, a segment of Colorado's early history had been overlooked. Like scattered pieces of a puzzle, an article, a chapter, and a paragraph here and there provided clues and pieces of their story.

The more I learned about the Routts, the more I wanted to know. Soon I was deeply involved in extracting the details of their story from libraries, historic sites in Illinois and Colorado, family descendants, and cemeteries. In these early stages of research, I visited Riverside Cemetery.

When I arrived at the cemetery, I stopped at the manager's office to pick up a map and a booklet that described many of the Colorado pioneers and early public figures of Denver buried in the cemetery. The booklet provided instructions for a self-directed walk. The Routt family plot was the second stop on the history walk. A large granite stone with "Routt" carved boldly on it loomed over smaller headstones of family members. I took my time looking at each stone and studying each inscription.

Eliza's and John's headstones lie side by side in the shadow of the large family stone. *Eliza F. Routt 1839–1907* was inscribed on one, and the other said, *John L. Routt 1826–1907*. How interesting that they had both died in the same year, I thought. Headstones for various descendants surrounded the family stone, and I carefully recorded the information for genealogy notes.

I did not hurry to leave. Instead, I loitered near Eliza's stone, soaking up the sunshine and thinking about similarities between Eliza's life and my own. Like me, she had been born and raised in central Illinois. After her marriage in 1874, she traveled to Washington, D.C., then to Colorado, a century ahead of me. In her time, she traveled by train and horse-drawn coach. After my marriage in 1974, I arrived in Colorado with my belongings in a Volkswagen.

When Eliza came to the western territory of Colorado from Illinois, the Civil War had been over for just a decade, and the new territorial capital was reeling from the growth that the discoveries of gold, then silver, in the mountains had brought. It must have been a substantial challenge for a Victorian lady to become a

Woman of the West, to thrive, and to pursue progressive causes in such a wild and unsettled place.

When I came to Colorado, the nation was recovering from the aftermath of the Vietnam War and there was a gasoline shortage. One thing Eliza and I had in common a century apart, other than our heritage, was that we were both newly married and eager to start life in the West with a new husband.

Overcome by a strong desire to know more about the Routts, I said, "Eliza, talk to me." How foolish I felt when I realized I had spoken out loud. Fortunately, there was nobody close by to hear.

Of course, Eliza did not speak to me that day from the grave. However, over the next several months, she shared the story of those exciting early days of Colorado through books, photos, newspaper articles, documents, manuscripts, receipts, and love letters.

Fortunately, correspondence a century ago was handwritten, and we have museums, libraries, and archives to preserve those precious documents. However, the scope of any historical collection is limited by the items made available to and included in it. By writing a biography of the Routts, my intention was to collect as much information as possible so that historians or researchers who follow will have a foundation from which to work and to learn more about this important family and the times in which they lived.

With a lot of research and a little luck, Eliza spoke to me, presenting her story like a precious gift. There were discoveries and coincidences, which filled gaps and made their story come alive, revealing two people who worked in partnership to shape Colorado's history. As if by magic, books of documents fell open to just the right page, and letters buried in bulky files landed in my hands.

Once they joined together in marriage, the Routts combined their resources to perform public service resulting in important contributions to the community of Denver and the state of Colorado. *First Governor, First Lady—John and Eliza Routt of Colorado* is the story of those two lives—a forward-thinking activist and industrious Victorian lady named Eliza F. Pickrell, and her man, the irrepressible and engaging John L. Routt, last territorial governor and first state governor of Colorado.

This portrait of Eliza P. Routt, ca. 1874, hangs in Routt Hall, Colorado State University. *Courtesy Colorado State University*.

1

The Pickrell Pioneers

When a little girl from Illinois became a prairie orphan early in life, nobody could have guessed that she would grow up to lead the women of an entire state. Perhaps it was fate that led Eliza Pickrell to fall in love with an ardent politician named John Routt who would respond to the lure of the West.

When they met, Routt recognized in Eliza her many fine, sensible qualities, which would help them maintain their stability while they worked together to build the new state. In a letter written while he was courting her, John wrote to Eliza, "I confess that I am unable to find words to express to you my admiration for your exalted character, or to describe my feelings of affection for you."[1]

Of course, at the time, John Routt was not aware of his destiny. His goal was to be with the woman he loved and to convince her of his suitability as a husband. This was expressed in touching terms when John wrote to Eliza, or "Lila" as she was called by those closest to her, as they planned their marriage. In a letter dated April 9, 1874, John wrote:

> I am delighted to know that you are "satisfied, settled and happy" and although you have known me but a short time, yet you are willing to believe that "I will always be kind to you" and you say that if I am that you will be happy. This is all that a reasonable man could ask of a Lady. I trust that you may never have cause to change your opinion of me. For if I know

> my feelings, God knows that I wish our union to be a happy one—and I shall try to make you a considerate, devoted and loving husband, and I have no doubt but that you will make me a devoted wife, and loving companion …
>
> When persons marry they take some risk of course, but we have arrived at an age when we ought to be able to determine the kind of a person we wish for a companion. So darling, we must look to the future *trustingly*.[2]

Although John Routt did not yet know that his political and business aspirations would lead him to Colorado Territory, he did know that he would need for his partner a woman who could provide a loving foundation and stability. He admired a woman who was brave, intelligent, and independent, with interests and aspirations of her own. Maybe, as it was said, the silver miners of Colorado needed one wife to help them through the early struggles to achieve their riches and another wife to help them enjoy their success, but the author of that idea did not know Eliza Routt.

Eliza Franklin Pickrell was born into an intrepid pioneering family on the newly settled prairie of central Illinois in 1839, 1,000 miles east of Denver City, the territorial capital of Colorado, where circumstances would later lead her as the wife of John Routt. Eliza's grandparents, Abel and Sarah Pickrell, were married in 1804 in Montgomery County, Kentucky. They bought land there, their children were born there, and from there Abel Pickrell was dispatched to fight in the War of 1812. It was their home until 1818 when they moved on to Shelby County, Kentucky.[3]

The first of their six children to travel from Kentucky to Illinois was the oldest son, Eliza's uncle, Jesse Alexander Pickrell, who left in 1828. Jesse was searching for fertile prairie land to settle and farm. He found it in the rich soil of Sangamon County, Illinois, near the capital city of Springfield. The area was still wild and unsettled, but Jesse saw great potential for prosperous farming and a new community. Optimistic about the future, Jesse rode back to Kentucky in the spring of 1830 to fetch his brother William.

Returning to central Illinois together in the fall, the Pickrell brothers had only three horses and $300 (or $100 if family lore is to be believed) between them. They set off to buy land on which to start a new life and a new community, and raise their crops and families. In the fall of 1831, their parents, Abel and Sarah, followed them to Sangamon County, traveling with their daughter, Mary Ann, and another son, twenty-year-old Benjamin Franklin Pickrell. Benjamin settled down to farm and bought land in 1832 and 1833. Abel and Sarah's son, Oliver, had died in 1829. Their daughter, Eveline, married and stayed in Kentucky for a few more years.

The Pickrells were hardworking and industrious farmers who raised crops and livestock, often using innovative methods such as importing new breeds of cattle to the area. As they settled into farming the beautiful Illinois countryside, they helped build a community they named Mechanicsburg in which they would become prominent citizens and agriculturalists. The name came from a plan devised by William Pickrell in 1832 to lure mechanics to the area. A plot of land was offered to any mechanic who would pay for the land title and build a house on the plot. The town was built around a square set aside for a public park.

When the need arose for church services, school classes, or a postmaster, the community-minded Pickrells went to work and made it happen. The first church services in the area took place in Jesse Pickrell's home. The family became involved in education, public service, and politics.

Among the Pickrells' friends was another pioneer from Kentucky named Abraham Lincoln. At the time, Lincoln was a lawyer, legislator, and a rising star on the local political scene. He wrote letters to the Pickrells, asking for their help in getting the vote out as he campaigned across the state, building political support for the Whig Party. After saying he was "much obliged" for their help, these letters were signed, "Your friend as ever" or "Yours as ever, A. Lincoln."[4]

Benjamin Pickrell courted Mary Ann Elkin, and they were married on October 5, 1834. Mary Ann was one of nine living children of Elizabeth E. Constant and William F. Elkin, who had recently arrived from Xenia, Ohio. Benjamin and Mary Ann began farming along with the rest of the Pickrell family in Sangamon County, and started what promised to be the beginning of a large family of their own. They had two sons, William Thomas born in 1836, and Francis Marion in 1837.

Unfortunately, their lives together would not last long. Benjamin died on August 28, 1838, at the age of twenty-seven. Jesse would later honor his memory by giving one of his own sons the name Benjamin. At the time of his death, Benjamin's young wife was pregnant. In the middle of winter, on January 30, 1839, a baby girl was born to the frontier widow who already had two boys to support. The baby was named Eliza Franklin Pickrell.

While Eliza was still an infant, her mother remarried on October 4, 1840, to a man named Abner Riddle. They had a child of their own in December 1841 who they named Hamilton Rush Riddle. He grew up to become a successful doctor in Sangamon County.

A few months after giving birth to her son with Abner, Mary Ann died on March 9, 1842. After the deaths of both Mary Ann and Benjamin, the Sangamon County Court appointed Eliza's uncles Jesse and William Pickrell as guardians of Eliza and her two brothers. Each child was awarded $300 from their father's estate.[5]

Eliza's uncles had large families of their own, and little Eliza was sent to her maternal grandparents to be brought up in their home near the capital city of Springfield. Her grandfather, Col. William F. Elkin, was a veteran of the Black Hawk War and an Illinois state legislator. He and his wife, Elizabeth, had nine children of their own, most of them still living at home.

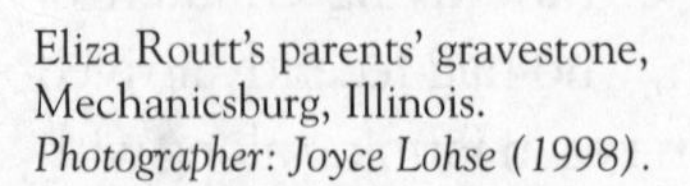

Eliza Routt's parents' gravestone, Mechanicsburg, Illinois.
Photographer: Joyce Lohse (1998).

Eliza blended into their busy household. She was too small to fully understand her tragic loss and was welcomed into her grandparents' hearts, lives, and home.

The Elkins had come to Illinois from Ohio through Indiana in 1825 and settled on wild prairie land eight miles north of Springfield on Fancy Creek, where they started their farm. William Elkin was elected sheriff in 1840 and re-elected in 1842. Called "a kind and true man" in his obituary, he served on the Sixth, Tenth, and Eleventh General Assemblies in Illinois. He was a member of the "Long Nine" Delegation, a group of nine men, which included Abraham Lincoln. This nickname was adopted because of their collective height as well as their political stature. Added together, the total physical height of the delegation was fifty-four feet, led by Lincoln, the tallest, who measured six-foot-four.[6]

In this busy, political household in Illinois, Eliza grew up. The 1850 Sangamon County census shows William F. Elkin listed with his wife, and Eliza, listed as age eleven. In the 1860 Sangamon County census, William is listed with his wife, and Eliza, age twenty-one, among his household.

Eliza had no shortage of family members living close by. Her brother Francis showed up in the 1860 census as a twenty-two-year-old clerk living on his own. By 1860, Eliza's paternal grandfather, Abel Pickrell at age seventy-nine was living in the household of her Uncle Jesse, his wife, Elizabeth, and eight of their children.

Excerpts from a letter written in 1850 by Eliza's uncle William to his brother-in-law, Sanford Watson, who had traveled to Oregon, tells much about life and concerns in Sangamon County, as well as the lure of distant places.

Mechanicsburg, Illinois, March 18th, 1850

Dear Brother:

It is now near one year since you left Springfield, and we have not had a line from you. We are now anxiously looking for letters, as several have received them from friends who started with you last spring.

This leaves my family all well, and all of our friends and relatives in usual health so far as we know. I have not been out to hear much news, as my leg was broken over five weeks ago, and I am now just able to walk a little …

This has been an uncommonly warm winter. I have sown my oats and there is considerable plowing done.

The cholera, that much dreaded disease, did not reach us last year; it did not leave the watercourses and thoroughfares much. Samuel Baker died of it. The citizens of Springfield cleansed their city and I never knew it to be as healthy as it was last year.

Illinois is more prosperous than perhaps at any former period; the influence of the operation of the railroad has given a different aspect to things in the surrounding country, in the way of lumber especially …

Property is higher than it has been for many years. The inflatus of the California gold has found its way here. Mules are up to $100.00 and $120.00, oxen about $75.00, beef cattle on foot $4.00 to $5.00, wheat $1.00, flour $6.00. Lands have gone up from 20 to 50 per cent … lands are being improved and men are settling all about through the large prairies; but enough on this subject.

The gold mania has not subsided, it is thought by some that there will be a larger emigration to California this year than last, not many, however, from Springfield. I do not hear of many going to Oregon, though from the last accounts we get from there I should think the latter place the most certain for a fortune. A great many who went to California have returned and from what I can learn, two-thirds have come back poorer than they went. A great many have died …

Now, Sanford, if you have not already written anything in relation to your country, I wish you to do it, as we all feel more interested in Oregon than we used to. The distance does not seem so great as formerly and there are more inducements since you all are there. I should like to know how things did look to you, compared with what you expected.

I want to know the relative value of the country independent of the gold influence, for none of us know what that will produce. I want to know what Oregon can or will do in regard to her climate and soil, water and timber, etc., when it is all settled how much country can be cultivated to advantage and what it will produce? And what is the difference in value between the product of an equal acreage in these prairies and Oregon? What advantage would Oregon have in confining stock on the same number of acres, Winter and Summer? … I do not suppose that you can answer all these questions as fully now, or that you are as fully satisfied as to what the country is or how you will like it, as you will be after you remain in it longer, but you can form a pretty good idea from what you have seen and the experience of others. We want you to write every three months, and we will get it sometime.

Your brother
William S. Pickrell[7]

For all of his apparent interest in Oregon, William Pickrell never left Illinois, nor did his brother Jesse. Both are buried in the Pickrell Cemetery in Mechanicsburg, as are Eliza's parents.

The Pickrells and Elkins had large families, which were common among pioneers in the heartland who needed many helping hands on the farm. Relatives might have been scattered but were certainly plentiful, and the Pickrell family was close-knit. Eliza had plenty of cousins, aunts, and uncles nearby in Sangamon County.

By 1850, some of the Elkin children had grown up and moved away, but others were still in the house. Although they were her aunts and uncles, they became like brothers and sisters to Eliza. One of the Elkin sons, William F. Fletcher Jr., was only three years older than Eliza. Daughter Margery was almost seven years older. Eliza was particularly close to Margery, who married Edward A. Jones on July 1, 1852.

In 1867, the Elkin family, including Eliza, moved to Decatur, in Macon County, Illinois, where they resided in the Jones household. Eliza's grandfather, William, maintained his public position in the Register of Land Office in Springfield forty miles away until 1872.

According to the 1870 census, the home of Edward (age 32) and Margery (37) Jones included their daughters Luella (17), Ida (14), and Hattie (11), William Elkin (78), Eliza[beth] Elkin (72), Eliza Pickrell (28), and two servants. Eliza was born in 1839, but it appears she became three years younger for the 1870 census.

Four years later, thirty-five-year-old Eliza was about to meet and fall in love with John Long Routt, a forty-eight-year-old widower with five children, ranging from five to twenty-seven years old. Perhaps Eliza had yearned for the adventure and challenge offered by a life with someone like Mr. Routt. Or perhaps the familiar, cozy cocoon of family life and comfort was all she desired before he entered her life. Regardless of her attitude, marriage to John Routt would mean an end to the life she had always known and the beginning of adventures that would take her far from Illinois and her quiet life.

ENDNOTES

Chapter 1—The Pickrell Pioneers

1. John L. Routt to Eliza Pickrell, April 26, 1874, Colorado State Archives.
2. John L. Routt to Eliza Pickrell, April 9, 1874, Colorado State Archives.
3. Pickrell, Elkin, and Constant family histories from *History of Sangamon County Illinois*, Inter-State Publishing (1881), 1522; Joseph Wallace, *Past and Present of Sangamon County*, II (1904), 1638,1638–1643; Mildred Pickrell, *Descendants of Abel and Sarah (Taylor) Pickrell* (n.d.); W. W. Allers and E. L. Gochanour, *History of Mechanicsburg Methodist Church* (1986), 1; Edward J. Russo, *Prairie of Promise, Springfield and Sangamon County* (1983), 15; Paul Shelby, ed., *Historical Encyclopedia of Sangamon County* (1912), 157; John Carroll Power, *History of the Early Settlers of Sangamon County, Illinois* (1876), 566–568; abstract from Nathaniel S. Haynes, *History of the Disciples of Christ in Illinois 1819-1914* (1915), 586–587; B. F. Pickrell's land purchase record from the *Illinois Public Domain Land Tract Sales Database*, vol. 068, (121,164); and cemetery gravestones, Mechanicsburg, Illinois. Pickrell family history published in *Pickrell Peers* Newsletter, March 1981, vol. 4 (1), and June 1980, vol. 3 (2).
4. A. Lincoln to Jesse Pickrell, Nov. 3, 1859, from author's collection. Scott Spilky, "Learning About Lincoln at the University of Illinois," *Illinois Alumni*, (Sept/Oct 1999), 21.
5. Sagamon County, Illinois, Public Archives, Guardian's Case File Index 1825–1902, Case# 199, Benjamin F. Pickrell, 1840.
6. William F. Elkin obituary, Colorado Historical Society, Stephen H. Hart Library, MSS #977; Stefan Lorant, *Lincoln* (1969), 36 (photograph).
7. *Pickrell Peers* Newsletter (Dec. 1979), 65–67. Article notes that letter was previously published in the *Annals of Oregon.*

John Long Routt, ca. 1874, Washington, D.C., during his term as second assistant postmaster general. *Courtesy Colorado Historical Society, F-5202.*

2

John Long Routt

AS TRAGIC AND DIFFICULT as the Civil War years were for Americans, this period also provided pivotal and defining moments for many people. John Routt was one of those people.

John Long Routt was born on April 25, 1826, in Eddyville, Caldwell County, which became Lyon County, Kentucky. When he was just a toddler, his father, whose name was also John, died leaving his wife a farm to tend alone, four children to raise and feed, and limited resources.

The Routt family moved to Trigg County, Kentucky, in 1834 where John's mother, Martha Haggard Routt, remarried a man named Henry Newton. In 1835, the family moved to Hancock County near Carthage, Illinois, and in 1840, they moved to Bloomington, in McLean County, Illinois, where they settled.

John's schooling was spotty and his education was not fancy, but he understood the value of education at an early age. He was an insatiable reader and learned a great deal from reading at night in the family's humble cabin lit by candlelight and oil lamp. School for young Routt was in session only three months of the year, but whenever and however he could obtain books, he read and studied and learned on his own.

On August 1, 1845, nineteen-year-old John Routt married Hester Ann Woodson, who was born in Virginia in 1828. They embarked upon married life together with only $20 and a few belongings between them.

John worked for his cousin, Samuel B. Haggard, as an apprentice carpenter and machinist. For a short while, he worked in a wood mill and gristmill for a man named Mr. O. Covel where he earned 75 cents a day and learned to manage an enterprise. When the mill burned down, he resumed work as a carpenter.

Routt developed an interest in architecture. He studied and learned as much as he could since he had aspirations to pursue that as well. The 1850 Bloomington, Illinois census listed John with Hester Ann and their first son, three-year-old Francis [Frank], in the household and John's occupation as a carpenter.

In 1854, John Routt was elected alderman in Bloomington, Illinois, the first of his many political positions. He was a member of the Whig Party at that time, but soon after his election became a member of the newly formed Republican Party.

Through hard work, Routt was beginning to accumulate some wealth, although hard times came with the financial crash of 1856 and 1857. Routt also experienced a financial setback when land he had bought on the banks of the Missouri River was virtually washed away by a flood. The course of the river changed, flooding the rich soil along the banks of the river where Routt owned the bulk of his plot, rendering it worthless. Although he was developing a reputation as a shrewd and cautious financial manager, Routt did not show much promise as a successful investor or speculator at this point in his life.

Routt became township collector for McLean County in 1858. He was easily elected to two terms and in his honest manner was able to stabilize and take solid control of county finances, which had been poorly handled previously. His management skills increased along with his popularity and respect in the community.

A McLean County history, published in 1874, described John Routt as follows:

> In personal appearance, Col. Routt is slightly below the medium height, stoutly built, has a large, well-shaped head with prominent forehead, black hair, dark hazel eyes, and strongly marked features. He is courteous and affable, though firm and decided, and has a pleasing address,

> which wins him friends wherever he goes. His political common sense enables him to grasp a subject and comprehend it at once in all its bearings, and his decisions always promptly made, are, nevertheless, more than usually safe and correct. He reads human nature with remarkable accuracy, and seldom has occasion to revise his first estimates of character. He is ever ready to lend a helping hand to the worthy and deserving, but has a thorough contempt for all pretenders and shams, whether the shams be men or measures. There is not in Illinois, perhaps, among our active politicians, a more outspoken man or sincere friend, than John L. Routt.[1]

In 1860, John Routt ran for sheriff. While he was making the decision whether to run for the office, Routt learned that his opponent had said, "It would be folly for little Routt to run." He took this as a challenge and became determined with the hearty encouragement of his friends, and won the election handily.[2]

By the time the Civil War started, John Routt was a popular leader in Bloomington. On August 20, 1862, he resigned as sheriff, answering the call to arms by Abraham Lincoln, who had by then advanced from Illinois politics to become the country's president. Routt joined the Union Army at age thirty-six. He was paid a fifty-dollar bounty and was assigned the rank of captain.[3]

With his natural ability to organize and motivate people, Routt gathered together a company of men who became known as Company E of the 94th Illinois Volunteer Infantry, also known as the McLean Regiment. They were sent to Missouri for training.[4]

When Routt's company was sent into Arkansas from Missouri, he led them marching up the road singing, *The Girl I Left Behind Me*. The memorable march took three days and covered more than one hundred miles from Wilson's Creek battleground in Missouri to Prairie Grove in Arkansas, where they reinforced the troops. Although unharmed, Routt left the Battle of Prairie Grove with three bullet holes in his garments.

There were several verses and versions of the song, *The Girl I Left Behind Me*, written by Samuel Lover. This version was printed in *The Photographic History of the Civil War*, published in 1911:

The Girl I Left Behind Me

The hour was sad I left the maid,
a lingering farewell taking,
Her sighs and tears my steps delay'd,
I thought her heart was breaking;
In hurried words her name I bless'd,
I breathed the vows that bind me,
And to my heart in anguish press'd
the girl I left behind me.[5]

Routt's smallish, five-foot-two-inch stature was no handicap to him as a dynamic military leader, although he was said to have looked a bit comical next to his six-foot-three-inch orderly sergeant. What Routt lacked in height, he more than made up for with his dynamic personality and resourcefulness.

Under the leadership of Major General John A. Logan, Routt's regiment joined forces with General Ulysses S. Grant's men at Vicksburg. Grant's soldiers were cut off from their source of ammunition, which could be reached by crossing dangerous enemy territory. Grant had been told that obtaining the necessary ammunition was impossible, but without ammunition, his troops could not fight. Grant needed a good quartermaster who could get the needed supplies.

Grant expressed his dissatisfaction to Logan, who replied by telling Grant that although he was reluctant to give him up, he had just the man he needed, further testifying that this man was honest and above board. Grant responded by saying, "Send him along. It will be interesting to have such a man, though I am sure, Logan, that you have slipped up on this man somewhere. An honest quartermaster!"[6]

The man Logan sent to Grant was John Routt, who immediately volunteered to march with men, horses, mules, and wagons through the night, in spite of the peril, to obtain and deliver the badly needed ammunition and supplies. By the next morning, Routt had accomplished his mission with time to spare. Grant was impressed. Although Routt considered his part in the operation routine, Grant made a note of his name and never forgot what he considered to be a heroic effort.

In his position as quartermaster, Routt immediately raised the living standard of the troops, and he was promoted to the rank of colonel. On Grant's recommendation in the summer of 1863, President Lincoln commissioned Routt to be promoted to Assistant Quartermaster of Volunteers. He continued to serve in campaigns as far away as Louisiana and Texas until the end of the war.

After his army discharge in 1865, John Routt returned to Hester Ann, the "girl he had left behind" in 1862. In the years that followed, their family in their little home in Bloomington, Illinois, grew to include five children.

John Routt's Civil War commander and friend, Ulysses S. Grant. *Courtesy Ulysses S. Grant Association, Carbondale, Illinois.*

Upon his return to civilian life, John Routt was elected McLean County treasurer. He was easily re-elected after his first term for the outstanding job he had done by once again tidying up a messy county financial situation and restoring its good credit.

In the meantime, General Ulysses S. Grant was elected president in 1869 and was re-elected in 1873. When Routt's term as county treasurer was finished, his former general appointed Routt U.S. marshal of the Southern Illinois District. Grant's telegraphed message said, "I am simply putting you into that job to have my eye and hands on you, my friend."[7]

One of Routt's major tasks and accomplishments during this term was to direct the ninth census in 1870. Routt was a gregarious fellow. It is easy to imagine Routt and his assistants riding horseback through his district, with the heavy census book in their saddlebags, interviewing residents and farmers, recording their names, ages, birthplaces, and children, perhaps accepting a lunch or dinner invitation. Routt was presented with an award from the census bureau for his prompt and accurate handling and management of the census records.

The following year, Routt resigned as U.S. marshal when he accepted another appointment from President Grant, this time as second assistant postmaster general. Routt and his family immediately left their Illinois homeland for Washington, D.C.

In spite of the excitement and importance of his advancement in public office, Routt must have been shattered when in 1872, Hester Ann died. It was just over a year after his mother had died in Illinois. He was faced with the prospect of grieving his losses in the fast-paced national capital with his children, three of them still under the age of ten. His promising career in public office was suddenly overshadowed by the void left in his life and his heart by the death of his wife of twenty-seven years.

Two years later, John Routt had mourned and recovered to the point that he could move on with his life. He was not content to face the future alone, and it was time to take action. As a result, he arranged his first visit to Miss Eliza Pickrell in Decatur, Illinois.

ENDNOTES

Chapter 2—John Long Routt

1. E. Duis, *Good Old Times in McLean County, Illinois* (Bloomington, IL: Leader Publishing, 1874), pp. 858-863.
2. Ibid., p. 860.
3. John Routt's Civil War records found in U.S. National Archives record #1307. Illinois 94th Infantry described in Frederick H. Dyer, A *Compendium of the War of the Rebellion*, http://www.rootsweb.com/~ilcivilw/dyers/094inf.htm.
4. Albert B. Sanford, "John L. Routt, First State Governor of Colorado," *The Colorado Magazine*, vol. III (3), (August 1926): 81-86. Sanford was an acquaintance of Routt's during the 1890s.
5. Francis Trevelyan Miller, ed. *The Photographic History of the Civil War* (The Review of Reviews, New York), vol. 9, p. 349.
6. *The Daily News*, August 13, 1907, p. 2. Also, Henry Dudley Teetor, "Hon. John L. Routt, Ex-Governor of Colorado," *Magazine of Western History*, 9, no. 4 (Feb. 1889): 458-459 and Albert B. Sanford, "John L. Routt, First State Governor of Colorado," *Colorado Magazine* (August 1926): 81-82.
7. Robert Charles Voight, "The Life of John Long Routt" (master's thesis University of Northern Colorado, Greeley, Colorado, 1947). *Rocky Mountain News*, *Daily News*, *Denver Post*, *Denver Republican*, and *Denver Times*, (August 13, 1907), John Routt obituaries.

Eliza Pickrell Routt, age 37, shortly after the move from Washington, D.C., to Denver.
Courtesy Colorado Historical Society, F-33,689.

Two Make a Bargain

IN 1874, ELIZA FRANKLIN PICKRELL at age thirty-five was mature, solid, sensible, and unmarried. She had grown up in the home of her grandfather, a military man and state legislator, in whose household she had grown accustomed to the decorum and protocol required of a politician's family.

Her grandmother, who had died two years earlier, guided Eliza's upbringing along with that of her own children through the height of the Victorian era. Eliza had thus made the transition from a pioneering background to a cultured life. She was educated, had traveled to Europe, attended the opera, learned to sew on a machine, and developed an extensive social circle of friends and relatives in Illinois.

Eliza Pickrell and John Routt, both of upstanding reputation, had known of one another but had never met. On one of John's visits to Illinois from Washington, D.C., a mutual friend named Mr. Dawson formally introduced him to Eliza. Shortly afterward in March 1874, John and Eliza began corresponding. In his letters, John addressed her as "Lila," a nickname used by family and friends throughout most of her life.[1]

Initially, the letters were stilted and proper. John and Eliza expressed in a roundabout way their mutual desire to become better acquainted, by extolling the importance of building lasting friendships. Eliza wrote that she wished to correspond, "in the hope that as we become better acquainted our friendship may be mutual, true, and enduring."

John responded in fervent agreement to Eliza's sentiment. He must have been encouraged and inspired by her correspondence. After some idle mention regarding the deplorable condition of muddy Illinois roads in the winter, John wrote of his immediate plans to return to Illinois to visit Eliza. He ended his letter by saying, "Hoping to see you very soon."

The visit must have been a success as Routt then addressed his letters from Washington to "My darling Lila" or "My dearest Lila" instead of "Miss Lila F. Pickrell," and he signed them, "your *best* and *most devoted and loving friend*, John L. Routt." He became anxious for her to write more often—twice a week, on Sundays and Wednesdays—and he promised to reply just as quickly, which he faithfully did. He fretted and became disheartened if his messenger arrived saying, "No mail from the West, Sir."

John Routt had suddenly become a gentleman in love, and he was lonely. He had mood swings during which his demeanor would visibly improve in his letters as he expressed his feelings for Lila and especially when he received a letter from her. He mentioned that because he had originally married at the young age of nineteen, it was only natural that he would be lonely during this period of separation, and he hoped Eliza would be patient with him.

John made little mention of his children in his letters, except once to describe to Eliza how he had helped his youngest daughter, Birdie, color Easter eggs, noting that Eliza would have laughed at his clumsy attempts. John's grown son, Frank, had accompanied his father to Washington. It appears that Frank and his wife, Kate, helped John with the younger children and the household, along with his trusted servants, Francis Bruce and his wife, Helen, who had also been his household assistants while his first wife was alive.

John also mentioned to Eliza that Mr. Dawson, who had introduced them, had been pestering him for details of their visits. He wrote, "I told him that I had to wait for the *distant future to develop the results of my visits with you*. I admitted to him that you treated me very nicely and that I was much pleased with you, and that I enjoyed my visits with you very much indeed. He seemed satisfied." He signed off with, "I remain your *best* and *most devoted* and *loving* friend, John L. Routt."

By the beginning of April, John Routt wrote to Eliza, "Now *my dearest Lila* I will close this uninteresting letter by assuring you of my anxiety to hear from you at least twice a week or oftener until the day designated by you when we are to commence life anew as husband and wife." The romance was moving along quickly, and plans for a future together were all but set.

John was soon reassured of Eliza's well being, and he was elated to learn of her reciprocal feelings. A tentative wedding date was set for May 21, 1874. In the flurry of letters that followed, John expressed his love for Eliza in proper, tender, and endearing terms as they made their long-distance, whirlwind plans to begin a new life together as husband and wife.

John and Eliza decided to keep their plans as secret as possible and worried a bit about public response to the announcement of their sudden alliance. They had many friends and relations in Illinois, and John's friends were especially anxious to see him remarry. He "threw dust in their eyes" by saying he was "ready to jump the broom stick but it takes two to make a bargain." John was eager to have Eliza by his side, and they both felt that their maturity allowed them to go forward with their marriage plans, without undo concern about public opinion or Victorian expectations of behavior.

In the correspondence that followed, John and Eliza did their best to get to know one another in a tentative way restricted by propriety and the great distance

Francis T. Bruce, Routt family friend and servant. Bruce and his wife moved from Washington, D.C., to Denver with the Routts. *Denver Post*, August 14, 1907.

between them. John was excited, anxious, and sometimes impatient for their wedding day to arrive, which he attributed to his "ardent nature." He sometimes grew melancholy in his loneliness and comforted himself by reading her letters repeatedly and replying with his tender words of love and hopes and plans for their future together.

With Congress still in session, John fretted that he would be unable to take as much time away from his work as second assistant postmaster general as he would have liked. Routt had originally hoped that he and Eliza would be able to travel to California on their wedding trip. Instead, they would take the train from Springfield, Illinois, to St. Louis, Missouri, for a visit before going on to Washington, D.C., to move into his home there. Routt was concerned whether this plan would be acceptable to his new bride.

Eliza's response to the change in plans was to say, "Of course if we cannot go to California now, I shall be entirely satisfied. Do exactly as you think best, and if it is necessary for you to remain in Washington, I would be perfectly willing to go there direct, as it would seem very nice to go *home* direct, or if it would suit you better to take the trip, and would prefer deferring our marriage until after the Adjournment of congress, I am perfectly willing for that."

Eliza's practicality and understanding of John Routt's situation endeared her to him all the more. In his response, he said, "You are such a *dear good girl* and I appreciate your kindness & generosity in being thus considerate. For I assure you that but very few ladies would have been so considerate and generous about a matter of this kind. I cannot think of postponing our *marriage* beyond the 21st of May, for I am so anxious to have you with me—and I do not apprehend any difficulty in getting away then—but my only fear is that I cannot be away very long—Still I am calculating on going to California if possible. But my *dear good Lila*—if we cannot get to go there *now*, we will try & do the next best thing & I shall leave it for you to determine what course would suit you best. We will write more on this subject."

They wrote of future plans for a trip to "Denver City" when John had more time to travel. This indicates that both John and Eliza had a strong desire to visit Denver City. It is possible John was intrigued by the stories coming from Colorado about mineral strikes. At the time, gold strikes in California and other western states were widely covered in newspapers, and the excitement lured many adventurous Americans westward.

Eliza busied herself preparing for the wedding, but revealed the impending wedding plans to only a few close friends and relatives. She made a trip from Decatur to Sangamon County for her last visit as "Miss Pickrell." John assured her he would do all he could to help her plan visits with family and that he placed a high value on family relationships.

John complimented Eliza on her discreet handling of the wedding plans. She revealed to him that she had always been "quiet and undemonstrative in nature." He pointed out that economy in the use of words was an asset and that she had demonstrated that she was a warm and loyal person who placed a high value on her relationships.

Frank and Kate Routt in Washington, Eliza's grandfather in Decatur, and Eliza's Aunt Margery and her husband, Edward Jones, quietly helped the couple plan their wedding ceremony. A "Miss Lucy," possibly Margery Jones's daughter, Luella, was mentioned in correspondence as a good friend and confidante who strongly approved of Eliza's choice. John mailed his outline for an "at-home" card for Eliza's approval before having it printed.

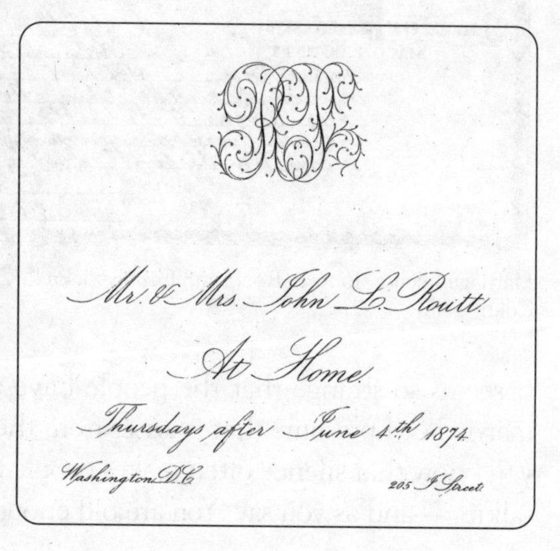

Mr. & Mrs. John L. Routt

At Home

Thursdays after June 4th 1874

Washington D.C. 205 I Street

John Routt relished springing the good news on friends. He planned to telegraph their wedding announcement to newspapers from St. Louis. As he put it, "I do hope that we will be able to surprise everybody & especially the Bloomington & Springfield people—

MARRIAGE LICENSE

STATE OF ILLINOIS
MACON COUNTY

THE PEOPLE OF THE STATE OF ILLINOIS.

To any person legally authorized to solemnize Marriage

GREETING

You are hereby authorized To join in the Holy Bands of Matrimony and to celebrate the Rites and Ceremonies of Marriage between Mr John L. Routt and Miss Eliza F. Pickrell according to the usual custom and laws of the State of Illinois and you are required to return this License to me within thirty days from the celebration of such Marriage with a Certificate of the same appended thereto and signed by you under the Penalty of One hundred Dollars

Witness Henry W. Waggoner Clerk of our said Court and the seal thereof, at his office in Decatur in said County this 21st day of May A.D. 1874

H. W. Waggoner
County Clerk

STATE OF ILLINOIS
MACON COUNTY } s.s.

I John W. Tyler a Minister of the gospel hereby certify that on the Twenty first day of May 1874 I joined in Marriage Mr John L. Routt with Miss Eliza F. Pickrell agreeably to the authority given in the above License & the custom & laws of this State. Given under my hand and seal this Twenty first day of May A.D. 1874

John W. Tyler seal.
Eld of the Christian Church

Marriage license, John L. Routt and Eliza F. Pickrell. Office of the County Clerk, Macon County, Ill.

It seems so strange that the people have an idea that you are to be married & I presume that it arises from the fact you say nothing—for you know that silence often makes people more suspicious than much talking—and as you say 'You are old enough to marry'."

Routt candidly apologized for being "boyish." His plainly stated wish was for a companion who would sympathize with him about the cares of the day and who would share with him his hopes for a happy future together while promising always to be kind and caring. As the wedding day drew closer, he wrote, "I think of you, all the time, and I will be so happy when you are home with me in our own home."

The flurry of correspondence ended with a short note from John to Eliza as he prepared for his trip to Illinois to be married.

Washington, D.C., May 16th 1874

My Dearest Lila,

It is most train time and I am about ready to start to the Depot. I have nothing special to write my *darling girl* this afternoon except to tell you that I am very happy and I feel as if I was to see my future companion very soon.

I trust that you feel as contented and happy as I do and I most earnestly hope that as we become better acquainted with each other – that our attachment and affections may become *very, very strong* and *ardent* and that our future may be full of *Joy* and "*Sunshine.*" I have just time to write you these few lines, so you will please excuse this tiny note.

Hoping to see you *Tuesday* next, I remain Your Most Devoted and Loving Friend,

John L. Routt

On May 21, 1874, Eliza F. Pickrell and John L. Routt were married in Decatur, Macon County, Illinois. John W. Tyler, elder of the Christian Church and minister of the gospel officiated at the ceremony. The certificate witnessed by Henry W. Waggoner, county clerk, stated, "You are hereby authorized to join in the Holy Bands of Matrimony and to celebrate the Rites and ceremonies of Marriage between John L. Routt and Miss Eliza F. Pickrell according to the usual custom and laws of the State of Illinois."

On the day of their wedding, the *Daily Republican* in Decatur, Illinois, ran the following notice:

On Thursday, May 21st, at the residence of E. A. Jones, Esq., 1½ miles north of the city, by Elder John W. Tyler, Col. John L. Routt, Assistant Postmaster General of Washington, D.C. to Miss Lillie [*sic*] Pickrell, of Decatur.

The newly married couple left on the noon train for Washington via St. Louis. The wedding ceremony was conducted in a quiet manner, without parade or display. The bride had been a resident of the city for several years, and was held in high esteem by all who knew her. The best wishes of the happy pair will attend them.[2]

A reporter for another newspaper quipped: "Col. J. L. Routt, Second Assistant Postmaster General and long a resident of Bloomington, was married last week to Miss Lela Picknell [*sic*] of Decatur. We trust the Col. will now enlarge the facilities of the mail service, as he has every opportunity to get up new Routts for the different departments."[3] Had that reporter done some homework, he would have known that John Routt already had five "little Routts." John usually enjoyed a good joke and no doubt appreciated this one.

Eliza's intelligence, proper upbringing and solid disposition, made her a fitting partner for the sincere and energetic politician, and equal to the challenge of managing his lively household. Although John was thirteen years older than Eliza, they were well matched. Both were mature adults of similar background who appreciated a quiet home life and the society of a few select friends. During their correspondence, he expressed his ardent love for her in endearing terms, which she reciprocated, and both exhibited that key ingredient for a good relationship: a sense of humor.

Leaving Illinois for Washington was no small matter for Eliza. Not only had her family pioneered and settled the area, but she was leaving behind a formidable number of friends and relatives, with relationships deepened because she had been orphaned so early in life. However, she was ready to establish a family of her own while maintaining that Pickrell pioneering spirit within her heart.

Eliza was no doubt prepared for a change and a challenge. In John, she had found an honest, hard-working, and spirited partner who was eager to share his life and affection with her and would make her life forever interesting. Eliza would become his anchor, keeping him on course with his duties and aspirations during his political career and business endeavors, while nurturing her own interests and goals.

After the wedding, John dropped the formality and pretense in his notes to Eliza. In one note, he asked Eliza to have their coachman, Bruce, bring their coach around in the afternoon to give Mrs. Senator Logan a ride to the depot. In another, he mentioned that a friend, a general formerly from Illinois, would be coming by the house to visit later. He addressed his notes to "My Dearest 'Baby' " and signed off with "Your Loving 'Boy' – JLR."

The marriage was off to a good start. John and Eliza had quickly entered into the intimate, easy comfort of loving married partners. Their home life commenced at No. 205 "I" Street in Washington, D.C., where Eliza took charge of domestic duties, while John continued his position as second assistant postmaster general.

Routt had maintained a relationship with General William T. Sherman and his wife, Ellen, from Civil War days. The Shermans lived at 207 "I" Street, next door to the Routts. The Shermans were not only the Routts' friends and neighbors, but were also their landlords. It was to them that John and Eliza paid rent.

A year after the Routts' arrival in the capital city, President Grant once again guided their lives in a new direction. Grant, who had been elected to a second term, sometimes stopped to visit with Routt at the Post Office Department. From these visits, Grant learned that Routt was restless and had a strong desire to go west to Colorado Territory. Soon after, Routt got his wish. Grant rewarded John for his years of dedicated government service by appointing him governor of Colorado Territory.

The prospect of life in Colorado Territory must have been both exciting and daunting for the Routts. Their destination was Denver City, as the new capital was called until 1874, when "City" was dropped from the name. It was barely settled. Following the first influx of '59ers, get-rich-quick miners seeking gold in Colorado in 1859, during the decade between 1860 and 1870, the population hovered just below 5,000 people. With the arrival of the railroads and the discovery of silver in the mountains, the population of Denver exploded by 700 percent, to 35,629 residents by 1880.

Three railroads completed routes to Denver in 1870. The Denver Pacific from Cheyenne, Wyoming, and the Kansas Pacific, from Kansas City and beyond were the first railroads to affirm Denver's importance by their presence. The Denver and Rio Grande was built soon after, with its narrow gauge route south along the front range of the Rocky Mountains. By the mid-1880s, there were 100 trains a week traveling into Denver.

With the advent of railroad traffic came travelers, tourists, pilgrims, and prosperity. Denver provided a starting point, a bustling, polluted, noisy, rowdy crossroads for those who came west to seek their fortune. Many train travelers came motivated by the search for riches in the mining camps, while others came to farm the semiarid land, building extensive irrigation ditches and braving grasshopper infestations and residual threats of raids by displaced American Indians.

Some train travelers were pleasure and health seekers, lured by the fresh mountain air and the beautiful mountain landscapes. Pioneer photographer William Henry Jackson produced beautiful landscape photos during the Hayden Surveys of 1873, 1874, and 1875, which were used extensively to publicize the railroad companies and to lure tourists to Colorado.

In 1875, the Routts traveled across the wide continent to their unknown future in Denver, the Queen City of the Plains. The trip by train was most likely long, tedious, and uncomfortable. Delays due to obstructions and washouts along the train tracks were expected. In spite of its flaws, train travel was a luxurious improvement over the long, treacherous wagon journey of pioneers just a few years before.

The Routts arrived in the wild, young city of Denver only a few days before his inauguration. John prepared quickly to assume his new position as territorial governor of Colorado with Eliza at his side as Colorado's first lady.

ENDNOTES

Chapter 3—Two Make A Bargain

1. Hand-written letters from John Routt to Eliza Pickrell (1874), Colorado State Archives, file #9353.
2. *Daily Republican* (Decatur, IL) May 21, 1874. Colorado Historical Society, Stephen H. Hart Library, MSS #977.
3. Colorado State Archives, file # 9353.

Governor Routt, ca. 1876. *Courtesy Colorado Historical Society, F-4872.*
Photographer: C. Bohm.

4

The Centennial State

COLORADO CITIZENS viewed their new territorial governor with cautious optimism tinged with suspicion. They needed a strong leader to unify them on the issue of statehood, then lead them to attain it. Routt's predecessor was Edwin M. McCook, another Civil War veteran appointed by President Grant. McCook had misused his power and position, causing Coloradans to protest his appointment. They also felt that their territory was being used as a dumping ground for carpetbaggers and inept politicians. Colorado had had seven appointed territorial governors slide in and out of office during the fifteen years since 1861. The unpopular McCook was removed from office, but was later reinstated—to the dismay of the public—until he was removed for good in 1875. Citizens were skeptical that Routt might be yet another carpetbagger, an outsider sent from Washington to merely smooth over the resulting rift of distrust in the state and in the Republican Party.

Routt had the support of the local press. The *Rocky Mountain News* welcomed "a new era of honesty and good government inaugurated." Two weeks later, the same newspaper printed, "Your people may congratulate themselves on the chance or good luck of having Colonel John L. Routt to serve them. No exception can be taken to him other than that he is not a resident of the territory. When the people of Colorado come to know him as does your correspondent, they will not only like him as a man and officer, but respect and admire him as a citizen."[1]

Glowing reports of Routt's reputation continued in an effort to reassure the suspicious residents of his good intentions: "He leaves his present place few enemies and many warm friends who regret his departure, and he goes without the smell of fire on his garments which is not always the case with persons placed in the position he has occupied. No man ever accused Routt of taking a dollar that did not belong to him. He has fair ability, and a splendid education, large experience in public matters, and is a good executive officer."

Another testimonial stated, "His integrity is perfect. As a man, he is genial and generous. I greatly regret his departure from the city, but I know that he will so conduct the affairs of his new office as to give high satisfaction to all the candid people of Colorado, and to confer upon them substantial good."

Routt was ready to roll up his sleeves and go to work to transform Colorado from a territory into a state with full representation in Washington, and to embrace it as his family's new and future home. When the Routts arrived in Denver on March 21, 1875, they took up residence at the fashionable Inter-Ocean Hotel. In the years 1876 through 1879, the Routt family lived at 373 Lawrence in 1876, the Alvord House at Larimer and Eighteenth Streets in 1877 and 1878, and at 330 California in 1879.

John Routt's gregarious nature made it easy to connect with his new community. He communicated easily with laborers, professionals, or politicians, and set about resolving their political differences. He exercised his natural problem-solving skills to address the qualms of Colorado's citizens about statehood as he attempted to unify factions. To satisfy the public that he had Colorado's best interest in mind, Routt explained at a reception, "I was getting ready to come and make my home in Colorado anyway."[2] He further declared his long-term commitment to Colorado by stating that he and his family wished to settle in as citizens and engage in private pursuits once his term had expired.

On March 29, 1875, John Routt took his oath of office as what would be Colorado's last territorial governor. The oath was administered by Judge Hallett at the Wells Fargo Express Company Building, located on the southwest corner of Fifteenth and Market Street, then known as Holladay Street, in Denver.

The first hurdle for the new administration was to develop an acceptable constitution under the Colorado Enabling Act, which would allow Colorado to become a state. Thirty-nine delegates were elected to draft a constitution, then screened and certified by Routt and other public officials. In December 1875, they embarked upon the daunting task of developing a workable constitution. The delegates scrutinized constitutions from other states and used them as a model to improvise their own document. It took several months for the committee to create and agree upon a workable draft. Routt acted as an observer of debates and deliberations until delegates finally voted and a majority of the committee accepted the new constitution.

Colorado's acceptance as a state by the rest of the country was not without resistance from eastern politicians, who considered Colorado much too wild and unsettled for statehood. According to one New York publication:

> There is not a single good reason for the admission of Colorado. Indeed, if it were not for the mines in the mountainous and forbidding region there would be no population there at all. The population, such as it is, is made up of a roving and unsettled horde of adventurers, who have no settled homes there or elsewhere, and are there solely because the state of semi-barbarism prevalent in that wild country suits their vagrant habits. There is something repulsive in the idea that a few handfuls of miners and reckless bushwhackers should have the same representation in the Senate as Pennsylvania, Ohio, and New York.[3]

A Philadelphia newspaper said, "Colorado consists of Denver, the Kansas Pacific Railway, and Scenery. The mineral resources of Colorado exist in the imagination. The agricultural resources do not exist at all."[4] Isabella Bird, a well-known traveler and author, reported her impressions of Denver in 1873 in her highly popular travel book, *A Lady's Life in the Rocky Mountains*. "At the top of every prairie roll, I expected to see Denver, but it was not till nearly five that from a considerable height I looked down upon the great 'City of the Plains', the metropolis of the Territories. There the great braggart city lay spread out, brown and treeless, upon the brown and treeless plain, which seemed to nourish nothing but wormwood and the Spanish bayonet."

Undaunted by heavy criticism from the East, the people of Colorado voted by a margin of 11,000 to ratify the constitution on July 1, 1876. Governor Routt certified the results and notified President Grant of the outcome. Statehood for Colorado was nearly complete.

On July 4, 1876, Routt acted as master of ceremonies at a grand Independence Day celebration in Denver that went on for two days. After a parade through the city, the celebratory gathering of city officials and exuberant citizens assembled in a grove on the banks of the Platte River near the Colfax viaduct. As he addressed the crowd, Routt was handed a telegram from Representative Stephen Decatur, who was attending the Centennial Exposition in Philadelphia. Carefully adjusting his wire-rimmed glasses, Routt read the words, "Are we a state?" from the telegram.

"We are!" was John Routt's immediate and emphatic, booming reply to the throng, who sent up a great, deafening cheer. He continued to read aloud his reply as sent to the Exposition. "The Centennial State and the twenty thousand here assembled send joyful greetings to the sister States of the American Union represented at Philadelphia on this glorious Fourth. (signed) John L. Routt." With that response, Colorado achieved the pride and dignity of statehood.

While Colorado was celebrating its status as the country's newest state in 1876, it was also celebrating the centennial birthday of the country. The coincidence inspired Colorado's nickname—the "Centennial State." On August 1, 1876, President Grant issued his proclamation of statehood officially making Colorado the nation's thirty-eighth state. That day is known as Colorado Day and is celebrated as the state's official birthday.

After a decade of negligible growth, Denver's population of less than 5,000 in 1870 was on its way to over 35,000 residents in 1880, exploding by more than seven-fold in just ten years. Colorado's capital city was growing fast. Colorado Territory's population jumped from 40,000 in 1870 to 194,327 in 1880 after statehood. The extent of Colorado's natural resources, agricultural potential, and natural splendor was just beginning to be discovered.

When Colorado became the thirty-eighth state, Routt's term as territorial governor came to an end. The state would have a new governor chosen by popular vote rather than named by appointment. Local politicians scrambled for the honor of being the first elected governor of the new state. Routt, who had already established himself as a trusted leader and who was committed to staying in Colorado, entered the race. He went to work by getting out and talking directly to the people.

Supporters considered John Routt's direct manner of speech an asset; his opponents did not always see it that way. His honest disposition sometimes caused him to speak more bluntly than some might have considered appropriate. For instance, if he observed an idle state employee, Routt would advise him in a most direct way to "fish, cut bait, or go ashore."

Once John Routt was selected as the Republican candidate, he faced the Democrat nominee, General Bela M. Hughes, in the general election. At one point, Routt's penchant for off-the-cuff oratory nearly cost him the election. In his first campaign speech, Routt said of his opponent General Hughes:

> I cannot soar so high as some of my friends of the other side, but I am short and spry, and when it comes to getting into the political pastures I can get in just as quickly as they by crawling through; perhaps I can beat them in, for they have to soar high to avoid the fences."[6]

A small, upstart newspaper, the *Denver Mirror*, published at the *Rocky Mountain News* offices by Stanley G. Fowler, was strongly anti-Routt. Fowler was inspired by the text of the speech to create and print a half-page cartoon lampooning Routt's ludicrous comments. A short, stubby Routt figure, with a carpetbag, was pictured trying to squirm between worn fence rails into the lush, political pastures of Colorado. His caricature, which was hung up in the fence, extended stubby arms through the rails.[7]

The *Denver Mirror* (September 17, 1876) ran this unflattering cartoon lampooning Routt's comment that he could win the election by crawling through the rails. The headline above the cartoon read: Colorado Vigorously Protests Against the Intrusion Upon Her State Grounds, of Fence Rail Crawlers and Red Headed Rooster Bipeds Who Want to Feather Their Nests With Congressional Eggs at Other People's Expense.

Encouraged by the stir the cartoon caused throughout the state, Fowler published a series of similar cartoons in *The Mirror* over the weeks leading up to the October election. Routt's supporters hurried to show them to John. Instead of reacting in anger, he burst into hearty laughter. "Ain't it too d__- funny for any use," he said.

Dismayed, Routt's advisors pointed out that the cartoons should be taken seriously before they turned the political tide just as he was getting a foothold with the voters. Routt responded by saying, "Don't worry. Send somebody over to the *Mirror* and buy the whole supply."

Anticipating that Routt planned to destroy all of the newspapers, his relieved assistants did as he asked and gathered up all copies they could locate. Destroying the newspapers was not Routt's intention. Instead, he gave orders that they be distributed at each meeting where he spoke as he campaigned around the state.

Routt's advisors were again horrified and responded by telling him that this would never do. He said, "It will have to do. Ain't it a good joke? Don't I know it is? I understand all that and I want

On October 1, 1876, the *Denver Mirror* again cautioned voters against voting for Routt. The original newspaper caption reads: Act with deliberation and judgment. Decide between Corruption in Office and Purity in Public Morals; the Restoration of Silver or Debasement of that metal; Brotherly Friendship and Co-operating or Sectional Hate; a Profligate or an Economical Administration. Eschew Strict Party Lines, and Vote as an Enlightened Conscience dictates, keeping steadily in view the Industrial, Educational and Moral Progress of the Centennial State, and the Best Good of the Entire Country.

people to laugh with me at it and I want to laugh with the people." The result was that the man who could take a joke and share it with the people won the election on October 3 and became the first governor of Colorado.[8]

Routt's political success also stemmed from his ability to win over his most cynical opponents. Soon after the election, Governor Routt paid a visit to the newspaper office of the *Denver Mirror*. Understandably, the publishers of the farcical cartoons were a little confused and apprehensive by the sudden appearance of the newly elected governor. The newspaper described the meeting as follows:

Gov. Routt came into our office on Wednesday, stumbling and stumping after that everlasting old cane of his. He was not in the slightest degree rabid, but with a smile as sweet as a full moon and a face as bland as a brass warming pan, gave us a friendly grip and assured us of his most distinguished consideration.

We expressed our sincere regret that Hughes was not elected, and we looked the disappointment we felt. But it was no use. What can you do with a man who laughs at cartoons of himself crawling through a rail fence and says they are "first rate" (his very words), "that he did say it, and thought it sounded pretty well at the time, though he found out his mistake when he saw himself quoted in the newspapers," etc. That "he entertained for us the warmest friendly feeling, just the same as though we hadn't fought him" (and he really spoke as if he meant it), "and he didn't care a — for the Kansas City *Times*. Hughes was a fine old gentleman, Patterson a man of splendid abilities, etc." "He was coming up to see us often," and we expect if we should lock him out, he would burst the door in.

Now how can one resist such a person as that. He soon succeeded in thawing our rather awkward (at first) reserve, with his free and easy chat, and when he left, we mentally confounded the man, because we found it utterly impossible to dislike him. Routt has all the kindly elements of sociability and good nature, in which Hughes is somewhat deficient, while in culture, intellect and the higher attributes of manhood, the latter has by far the advantage of Routt.[9]

The quiet, low-key inauguration of Colorado's first state governor took place in a storeroom on Blake Street in Denver—one of the scattered provisional state offices. After Routt took his oath of office in a short ceremony, he walked up the street with a few friends to the statehouse, located in the three-story Chain & Hardy building on Larimer Street between Sixteenth and Seventeenth Streets.

Denver's Union Station, ca. 1894. *Courtesy Denver Public Library, Western History Department*, MCC-284. Photographer: L. C. McClure.

John Routt was ready to get down to the business of his new office. He settled in as a dedicated public servant who understood standards and priorities of those who worked with him. John P. S. Voght, a messenger assigned as a page to assist Governor Routt by delivering messages among the scattered state offices, remembered Routt this way:

> Exteriorly rough and brusque in manner and speech, yet within there was a kindly, and sympathetic heart; an abiding confidence in the good that is in men; a love for children and the greatest consideration for the children's welfare.
>
> He appreciated the weaknesses of boyhood for fishing and swimming, and often during the sweltering hot days of summer he would turn to me, saying, 'John, fishing or swimming ought to be good today?' Knowing his thoughts, I would timidly answer, 'Yes, I think so.' With an explosive 'D__- it, get out of here and have a good time,' without further ado I would leave space between me and the state house toward the Platte River.[10]

ENDNOTES

Chapter 4—The Centennial State

1. *Rocky Mountain News*, February 4, 10, 23; March 21 and 23; April 1, 1875 reported the Routts' arrival in Denver. See also, Richard D. Lamm, *Pioneers and Politicians* (Boulder, Pruett Publishing, 1984).

2. Albert B. Sanford, "John L. Routt, First State Governor of Colorado," *The Colorado Magazine*, III, no. 3 (August 1926): 81-86.

3. Theo. F. Van Wagenen, "Views on the Admission of Colorado in 1876," *Colorado Magazine*, III, no. 3 (August 1926): 87.

4. Ibid.

5. Mac Lacy Baggs, *Colorado: Crown Jewel of the Rockies* (Boston: The Page Company, 1918), 103.

6. *Daily News*, August 13, 1907, p. 6.

7. *Denver Mirror* political cartoons, September 3, 10, 17, 24, and October 1, 1876 (microfilm 126 at Norlin Library Archives, University of Colorado, Boulder, Colorado).

8. *Daily News*, August 13, 1907, p. 6.

9. *Denver Mirror*, October 8, 1876.

10. John P. S. Voght interview. *Denver Times*, August 13, 1907.

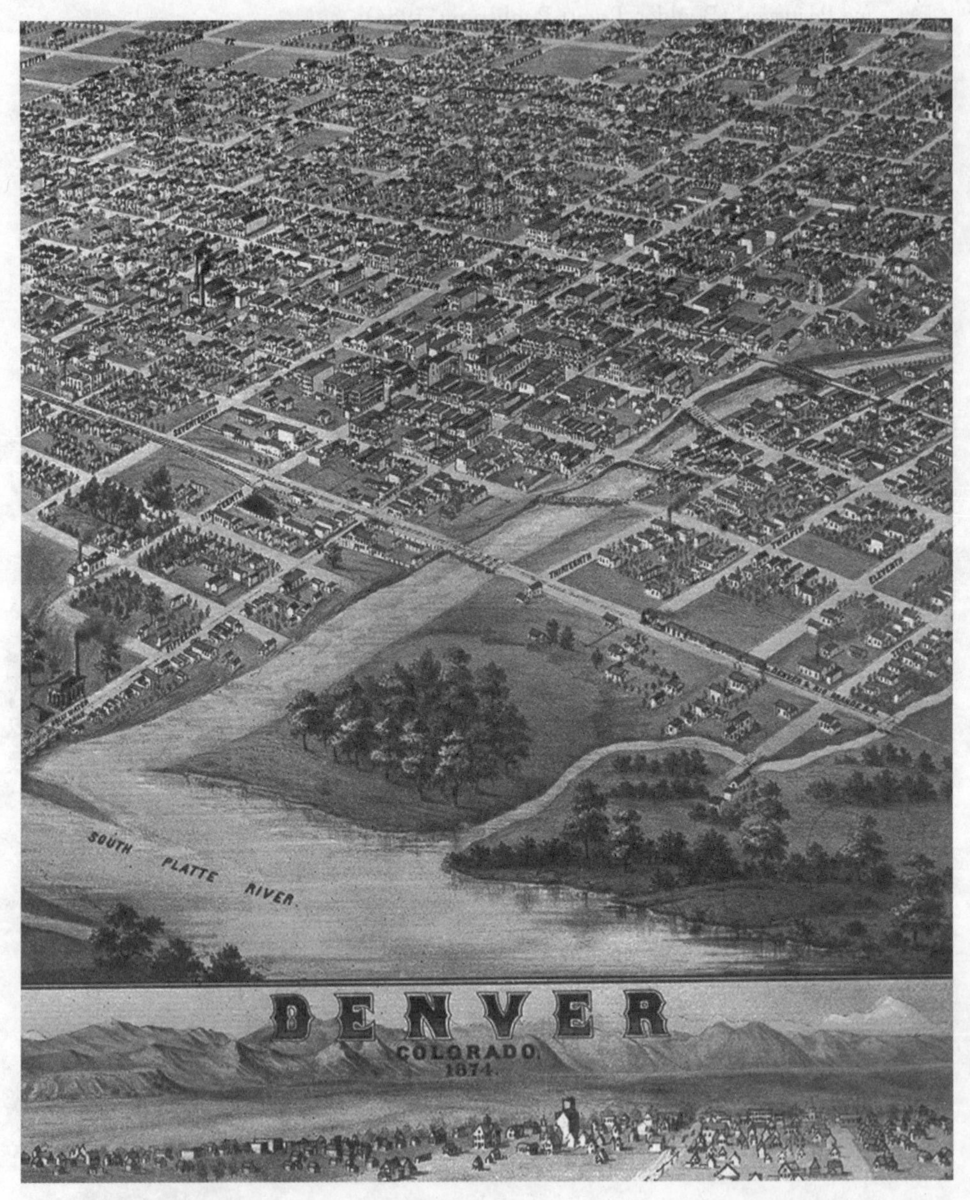

Denver in 1874, one year before the Routts' arrival.
Courtesy Denver Historical Society Library.

5

First Governor, First Lady

EXCITING TIMES WERE BEGINNING for the Routts. Little did John and Eliza realize, as Colorado became a state and they embraced their roles as first governor and first lady, that they were embarking on an endeavor that would greatly impact their family's destiny and the state's history. In the meantime, they settled into life in Denver City, a community still in the rough stages of becoming civilized. As first family, they saw it as their duty to set a high standard of conduct for future residents to follow.

John Routt described his assessment of prospects for business in Colorado, in a letter to a friend, which appears to be written on old territorial letterhead:

> Territory of Colorado
> Executive Department
> Denver, Dec. 5, 1876
>
> My dear friend:
>
> By reason of press of duties of 11th ultimo, has been thus far answered. I appreciate your congratulations and kind wishes and thank you for them. As to you coming to Colorado, I would say this:

> The country is very different from any in which I presume you have ever lived—the avenues to business are few and well filled, while strangers are constantly coming, who need employment. Our mineral resources, the chief support, are unlimited but they require capital for development. The best I can promise you at this time is that I will "keep my eyes open" and if I can obtain a situation for you on some of our railroads, will take great pleasure in doing so.
>
> I have letters similar to yours to answer daily and I never advise anyone to move here, without first taking a look at the country for himself.
>
> You may rest assured that I would be very much pleased to shake hands with you and welcome you as a citizen of our young and growing State.
>
> Very truly your friend,
> John Routt[1]

The new governor had his work cut out for him in helping to guide and shape the fledgling state. Routt appeared to have a good understanding of the state's economic situation, although his notion that mineral resources were unlimited was somewhat optimistic and naïve. However, while governor, carbonate silver lead ore mining was developed in Leadville, leading Colorado into a period of significant growth and wealth. Gold production had subsided, and the discovery of a way to process carbonate waste material to extract silver created a new frenzy of mining activity and excitement. Skirmishes over claims and land, as well as labor disputes, disrupted the peace. Colorado was becoming a lively place, and the governor had his hands full.

Meanwhile at home, Eliza Routt was busy managing the state's leading household. She had been through major changes in the previous two years. Life had been sedate and undemanding for her when she lived with her relatives in Illinois. After her rapid transition to married life with children in the nation's capital, her life abruptly shifted again when the family moved to Colorado.

As Colorado's first lady, Eliza Routt was expected to supervise the governor's household, become involved with the community, entertain official visitors, and set an example for the women of the state. Her competence as a natural leader allowed her to perform her duties in a most capable and proper manner. Eliza and her husband quickly became highly respected and well known for their gracious and generous hospitality, which extended far beyond Routt's term of office.

The late 1800s provided a unique set of challenges and standards for the first lady of Colorado. Sedate Victorian women were expected to work quietly in the background to provide a pleasant, hospitable home life, all the while remaining invisible. The daily life of women was restricted by the social limitations of Victorian graces as well as the physical constraints of Victorian clothing with tight bodices and long, flowing skirts. The result was women's home lives often lacked intellectual stimulation.

Eliza was determined to perform her duties as first lady to the best of her ability despite these restrictions. Further, she resolutely directed her intelligence into political activism and social change. Embracing such a progressive position required a delicate balance and was not easily executed.

Fortunately, for women in the western frontier, a certain amount of flexibility was allowed. In newly settled communities, women could exercise their independent spirit by writing some of their own rules and creating new traditions. Eliza was in a position to set an example for the women of her state. Accordingly and true to the high ideals of her nature, Eliza chose her alliances with caution and considered carefully the precedent she would establish for others to follow.

An August 1, 1926, retrospective article in the *Denver Post* about first families of Colorado described the expectations of Eliza's position and situation in quaint terms.

> Tho much of the formality of eastern entertaining was impossible in the new west, which had just begun to see the dawn of civilization, there were rigid, old-fashioned rules that had to be adhered to unless one would be

> classed with the riff-raff … Women were modest, retiring creatures, tho they had endured the hardships of the plains, and rugged pioneers who dared the 'wilderness' were of the old school of chivalry.

Another *Denver Post* article, "Wives of Colorado Governors," published November 11, 1902, explained that first ladies of Colorado were "women famed for hospitalities. Colorado has been exceedingly fortunate in the women who have held the social reins of the state coach. [Eliza Pickrell Routt was] capable and worthy of her lofty station. The Routt dispensation will long be remembered for its 'homelike' qualities. The 'glad hand' was extended to the country constituents at the capitol by 'Uncle Johnny' and a place prepared at the governor's mahogany for their refreshments by the first lady of the state."

According to the *Daily News* of Denver, Eliza did a fine job meeting the expectations set for her. "Mrs. Routt was the first mistress of the state's white house. On this account, she was sometimes referred to as *the Martha Washington of Colorado*."[2] Although described as regal in manner, Eliza performed her duties as first lady using the practical skills she had learned from her grandmother who also was the wife of a public figure.

John Routt had an amusing way of expressing his pride in Eliza. One day while he was working at his desk in the governor's office, some friends gathered and were loudly boasting about the size of fish they had recently caught. Routt continued to be occupied at his desk while the bragging escalated.

Suddenly, he looked up from his work and said, "Oh, what's the matter with you fellows anyway? I will bet money that none of you ever caught a fish half so heavy as I have. You fellows with your little ten-pound trout and twenty-pound catfish will have to take a back seat for me. Why, I caught a *Pickrell* that weighed 165 pounds—and weighs it today!"[3]

Routt's Pickrell joke had a history. During his courtship with Eliza, John had snuck in and out of her hometown of Decatur, Illinois, to visit her, hoping no one would notice. Ed Hill, his former deputy marshal in Bloomington, acknowledged his clandestine visits in a letter. As Routt reported it to Eliza, the deputy wrote,

"Colonel, do not flatter yourself, that you can come *West* and retire without some of your friends learning what you came out for. For my imagination, I can now see my former Marshal, not sixty, but forty miles away from Spring[field]. Putting on a clean collar of faultless cut, with his little boots polished 'to hill', he sallies forth with brightest sparkling eyes, cautions that he is going where—fishing—yes, fishing—some persons prefer *fish* of one species & some of another, but I imagine that the Col. is partial to *Pickrell*."[4]

John Routt's sense of humor was regularly exercised. By all accounts Eliza must have been a good sport to endure, and perhaps even condone, John's jovial tales, especially when she was the subject. The Routts were becoming a well-liked, popular couple in Denver.

During their first few years in Denver, the Routt family lived in temporary residences; the longest stay was for two years at the Alvord House at Larimer and Eighteenth Streets. They were far from wealthy. In Bloomington, Illinois, John Routt's holdings consisted of a two-story frame house and two lots worth about $2,500. He had earned only a modest salary as a public official there. Perhaps his modest lifestyle is why they did not purchase a house right away. Eliza must have anticipated the day when they would have a home of their own, befitting their position, where they could entertain guests of the state.

On New Year's Day 1877, their first social gathering as "His Excellency Governor Routt and Lady," took place at the state office on Larimer Street. The Routts, along with other newly elected state officials, prepared a large executive reception. It was their first opportunity to celebrate their position, and they decorated with splendor. The office facilities were bedecked with festive lights, a profuse display of flower and palm plants, and a banner in national colors with "A Happy New Year" emblazoned across it. A canopy of flags sheltered the overflowing and popular refreshment table.

More than a thousand people, representatives from nearly every town in the state, greeted the new Colorado officials and enjoyed the Routts' hospitality between eight and eleven o'clock that evening. One of Eliza's aunts from the Elkin family in Illinois was visiting and helped Eliza receive guests. The new administration was thus festively launched.

As they settled into their executive duties, John Routt was familiarly known as "Johnny" or "Uncle Johnny" to many of his associates. Albert W. McIntyre, who later was elected Colorado governor, once asked Routt how his wife should be addressed when he spoke to her. Routt told him, "I call her Lize, but perhaps you had better not be too d—- familiar, so address her as Eliza."[5] Eliza was known as "Lila" to those most familiar to her. John apparently chose not to divulge that personal detail to his colleague on this particular occasion.

John was a plain talker, prone to using colorful expressions and metaphors. He was aware of his limitations and kept his speech making to a minimum. However, his consistent directness also won him the loyalty of his constituents. Even the most straight-laced of the citizenry chose to overlook his weakness for swearing in favor of his honesty and personable charm.

On more than one occasion, Routt's awkward use of the language became a bit comical. His memory of names and faces was sharp, although he sometimes mixed them up. In one situation, the commissioners of Larimer County paid a call to the governor, bringing with them an architect named Quayle. After Governor Routt had been introduced to Mr. Quayle, Routt incorrectly addressed him as "Mr. Partridge." In response to this, Mr. Quayle politely corrected him by saying, "Quayle is my name, Sir." Routt responded by saying, "What's the difference? I knew it was some kind of d ____ d bird." Mr. Quayle answered to *Partridge* for the rest of the visit.[6]

Women's suffrage was a prominent issue in 1877, and Governor Routt was at the head of a long list of supporters published by the Denver press. Colorado's new constitution allowed women to vote only in school district elections. Eliza embraced the suffrage movement, giving her time, effort, and support to the fight for equal voting rights. Eastern suffragettes Susan B. Anthony and Lucy Stone traveled to Colorado to campaign and speak out for their cause.

In September 1877, Susan B. Anthony visited the mountain mining town of Leadville to make several speeches and to explain suffrage to the miners. Billy Nye's Saloon, the largest building in town, was chosen for one such assemblage. Miss Anthony braved the rough surroundings and tobacco smoke from the overflowing crowd to convey her message and educate the men in the saloon, remembering the experience later as quite an ordeal. The men had moderated their smoking for her benefit, but consoled themselves later with additional drinking.

Abner R. Brown recalled the scene in an address to the Society of Leadville Pioneers in May 1900:

> Nye purchased fifty yards of calico and tacked it over the entire bar, covering all the liquid attractions. He suspended business for the night in honor of his distinguished and strong-minded guest. The saloon and the back room were crowded to capacity, while there was an overflow crowd in the street. But the audience honored themselves and their guest by the most respectable attention.
>
> At the close of the lecture, Mrs. Anthony said that she deemed it necessary to give the audience some of the reasons why they ought to be liberal in their contributions and one of them was that her expenses up here and return were simply 'magnanimous'. Mr. Nye tells me that the gold rolled into the hat as it passed around not in nickels and quarters, but in nuggets and dust, from $1 to $3 to $5 apiece from many ill-clothed miners as they stood packed in the room. Some of them listening for the first time in their lives to the amazing power of oratory as it rolled fluently and sweet from feminine lips.[7]

Governor Routt was present at the gathering. To show his support and to help Miss Anthony be heard, he placed two barrels together and helped her stand on one barrel while he climbed up on the other to stand next to her and speak in favor of the cause. Later, he would share the Broadway Theater stage with her in Denver, further lending his support to women's suffrage.

In October 1877, suffragette Lucy Stone arrived from the East to speak to a large audience at the Lawrence Street Methodist Church in Denver. Even though suffrage workers campaigned hard to spread their message to the people of Colorado, the Colorado legislature voted it down soon after Lucy's visit by a margin of two to one. As a result, Colorado's Territorial Suffrage Association was disbanded, and supporters were encouraged to carry on the campaign individually for the next few years.

ENDNOTES

Chapter 5—First Governor, First Lady

1. John Routt to E. J. Smith, December 5, 1876. First published in the *Mark Twain Journal* (Kirkwood, MS) nd. Western History Manuscript Collection, Denver Public Library, WH 79, Box l.
2. *Daily News*, March 23, 1907.
3. *Denver Times*, August 13, 1907.
4. John Routt to Eliza Routt, April 19, 1874, recounting comments made to him by Ed Hill, Colorado State Archive #9353.
5. *Denver Times*, October 12, 1899.
6. *Denver Times*, October 12, 1899.
7. Don L. and Jean Harvey Griswold, *History of Leadville and Lake County, Colorado*, vol. 1, (Denver: Colorado Historical Society in cooperation with the University Press of Colorado) 1996: 145.

Harrison Street, Leadville, in 1879. *Courtesy Denver Public Library, Western History Department, X-471*. Photographer: George D. Wakely.

6

The Lure of Leadville

IN THE COLORADO MOUNTAINS, the Carbonate Camp exploded with activity and people, evolving into a community, which would become known as Leadville. The settlement boomed as miners poured in seeking wealth from the earth. Crowded and muddy, the town and its ability to provide facilities and supplies, such as food, lodging, and transportation, were stretched to the limit and beyond.

Population figures from the *Colorado State Business Directory* for Leadville tell part of the story:

1877	250	1882	20,000
1878	2,000	1883	20,000
1879	7,000	1884	20,000
1880	35,000	1885	20,000[1]
1881	15,000		

A century later, Leadville's population stabilized at around 4,000 people.

At its beginning as a mining camp in 1877, Leadville was a collection of six coarse cabins inhabited by a handful of people. It could be reached from Denver in one day of travel, partly by rail and partly by stagecoach.

The booming town had big problems. Prospectors with riches in their pockets were ready to spend. Gamblers and prostitutes arrived to help them part ways with their money in saloons and dance halls. Robbers and claim jumpers attempted to relieve the fortunate of their stakes.

When miners came to Leadville to find wealth by staking a claim, hillsides were clear-cut to make way for holes in the ground. Trees were hastily cut away to make room for mineshafts and to provide lumber for their construction as well as badly needed shelter and lodging. A dirty haze of smoke hung in the air from the zealous industry.

During the first strikes, miners found gold and dug away frantically at their claims, throwing aside the pesky black sand and carbonate material that got in their way. As the gold claims played out, the miners discovered that the carbonate material, which had been thrown aside all the while as waste, could be processed down to render precious silver. Suddenly, silver was the treasure of the day, and mining surged around Leadville in a renewed flurry of activity.

Leadville became a mecca for fortune hunters who arrived from all over the world with pans, shovels, and pickaxes. Many came by mule or horseback; some arrived on foot. Railroads competed with one another to be first to complete a direct line to Leadville to help move people and freight. The cost of riding the railroad, then stagecoach from Denver, was $16, plus additional charges for extra baggage, precluding anybody without cash in hand from traveling.

The town gradually met the needs of residents in many areas. In its first three years, Leadville had five newspapers and earned the reputation of selling the most newspapers for a town of its size in the world, keeping twenty-five newsboys busy selling from morning until night. In 1877, Miss Lottie Williams started the first Leadville school, which consisted of a two-month session of classes in a log house. The following year, school was in session for three months. Soon after, a high school was built for $3,000, and the school term was lengthened to nine months.

George Albert Harris, who knew firsthand about the lack of lodging, was responsible for single-handedly building the first hotel in Leadville. Arriving with fifteen cents in his pocket and unable to find a room, he spent his first night sleeping "curled up behind a log." Realizing there was an opportunity at hand, he built a rooming house called the City Hotel. Two years later, his City Hotel was described in the *Leadville Chronicle*:

> The first public house was commenced the 15th day of June, 1877, and was finished and thrown open to the public on the Fourth of July, nineteen days later. The builder and proprietor was Mr. G. A. Harris, the hero of this sketch. He performed every particle of labor in its construction, from the foundation to the roof. The side was ten feet wide by twelve feet long—a story and a half high. The first floor served as a dining room, office, kitchen, baggage room, parlor, reception room, etc., and the second or attic was used principally for lodging purposes. It afforded accommodation for eight sleepers at a time. The day was divided into three sleeping divisions of eight hours each. And thus the first hotel afforded sleeping accommodations for twenty-four guests, divided into three shifts of eight hours each.[2]

John was attracted to this wild place in the mountains. For most of his life, he had struggled to manage the public's finances responsibly, while his personal wealth remained somewhat marginal, if not lacking. Back in the Midwest, stories and rumors abounded about fabulous mineral strikes in California and Colorado. Like most of those who heard the stories, he was not impervious to tales of riches in the Rocky Mountains.

While visiting Leadville to observe firsthand the adverse conditions created by the mining boom on the community there, Governor Routt hoisted a pickaxe for the first time and succumbed to the prospecting bug. In a letter dated September 15, 1877, W. J. Palmer, president of the Denver & Rio Grande Railroad, wrote about the burst of mining activity in Leadville: "There was considerable excitement, and Senator Logan (the U.S. Senator from Illinois, 1871-1877) and Governor Routt were there, and out with picks, searching for ore."[3]

Senator John A. Logan had been Routt's commander in the Civil War—the officer who had reluctantly sent Routt to General Grant to fill the position of quartermaster. They stayed in touch and maintained their friendship after the war. When Logan came to Colorado for a visit, he traveled with the governor to Leadville. While there, they decided to do a little prospecting.

Soon after, in October 1877, John Routt was again in Leadville, this time with a mission. He hiked uphill to take a look at the Morning Star Mine, a twelve-foot-deep hole in the ground, which was for sale by the two men who had originally staked the claim, William Baldock and George Bradley. Routt climbed up Carbonate Hill behind Leadville and purchased the mine, "and closed the bargain," as he put it, "before coming off the hill."[4]

He must have been breathless by the time it was all over, unaccustomed as he was to the altitude of 10,200 feet on Carbonate Hill, and unaccustomed as he was to spending large sums of money. Some sources report that Routt paid $10,000 for the mine, an amount he surely did not possess. The quitclaim document for the transaction on file with the Lake County clerk states that the transaction was for $1,000, but this smaller sum may have been a down payment. Regardless, Baldock and Bradley were undoubtedly quite satisfied to be divested of their hole in the ground at any price.

The town of Leadville from Carbonate Hill in 1879. *Courtesy Denver Public Library, Western History Department*, X-498. Photographer: George D. Wakely.

Carbonate Hill, located adjacent to Leadville, was scarred by many similar holes, shafts, and rubble from miners digging through soil and rock, searching for rich mineral strikes. Some miners struck it rich, while others left penniless. Some who found their fortunes spent it on liquor in the saloons and fancy women in the dance halls of Leadville. Men like Baldock and Bradley grew tired of putting in enormous effort with no payoff. They had much to celebrate when they cut their losses by selling their claim and were liberated from any encumbrance it represented to them.

Between the price to purchase the mine and expenses to keep it running, Routt said he was, "down to real bedrock, and for a time, with my personal credit nearly exhausted, things looked as steaked [*sic*] as a corn basket, but I had faith in the ground and kept working at it."[5] He became preoccupied with making the mine pay off. It is easy to imagine that he would have put pressure on himself to prove the value of his investment, especially to his sensible wife, Eliza. Perhaps she was more than a little skeptical about his purchase.

Whenever time allowed, Routt abandoned the trappings and responsibilities of the governorship to ride the Denver and South Park Railroad and coach to Leadville. He was seen boarding the train, carrying only a small carpetbag, wearing miner's work clothes, with his jeans tucked into his boot tops in the style of a placer miner, and wearing a jacket stained with wax drippings from candles used for light in the mine. While he was in Leadville, Routt either camped outdoors or stayed in a rough mining cabin, working long shifts with his small crew of miners.

Routt's commitment to work the mine was no small undertaking. At that time, mines were dangerous places where lives and limbs could be lost in an instant. Cave-ins and explosions were common. Huge rock drills weighing over 300 pounds were aptly called widowmakers.

In later years, smaller, safer drills, which sprayed water to keep the rock dust down, became available. However, at the time of the Leadville boom, rock drills created a deafening, thunderous din, and raised constant clouds of rock dust. Many miners died of terrible, lingering illnesses caused by "dusted lungs," or silicosis, when sharp rock particles kicked up from the drilling and blasting equipment entered their lungs with each breath, shredding their lungs over time.

The miners must have appreciated that John Routt was willing to take the obvious risks to work long hours in the mine alongside them. After all, hired mine workers earned their wages, but it was the mine owners who collected the bonanza if they struck pay dirt.

Running the mine required a precarious balance of management of workers and expenses, assayers, and transportation of ore to smelters. Buying and selling ore in the mining camps was a science dependent upon the fair dealing and honesty of the mill men. John was able to keep close track of operations and save some expenses by pitching in with his own labor. This sacrifice and commitment to his stake kept him away from home for long periods of time.

Those days must have been hard for Eliza. She no doubt worried about John working in the mine while she stayed at home tending the lively family, with three young children ages eight through fourteen, as well as keeping up the household and community obligations while her husband was away. All their extra money was tied up in the Morning Star Mine—along with her husband's attention. It appears that John Routt was staunchly loyal to Eliza during their many years together, but the Morning Star proved to be a formidable mistress.

These circumstances did not prevent Eliza from becoming involved in the community while her husband's time and attention were occupied in Leadville. Organizations such as the Woman's Home Club, the Denver Orphan's Home, Colorado Woman's Suffrage Association, and Central Christian Church provided fulfilling diversions for Eliza. These groups benefited from her involvement for years to come and awakened her growing interest in public service.

The state legislature met alternate years, which gave Routt some leeway in his duties at the governor's office during his two-year term and allowed him to spend time to in Leadville. Although problems of state included the residual effects of economic depression in 1873, a grasshopper infestation, and continuing efforts to

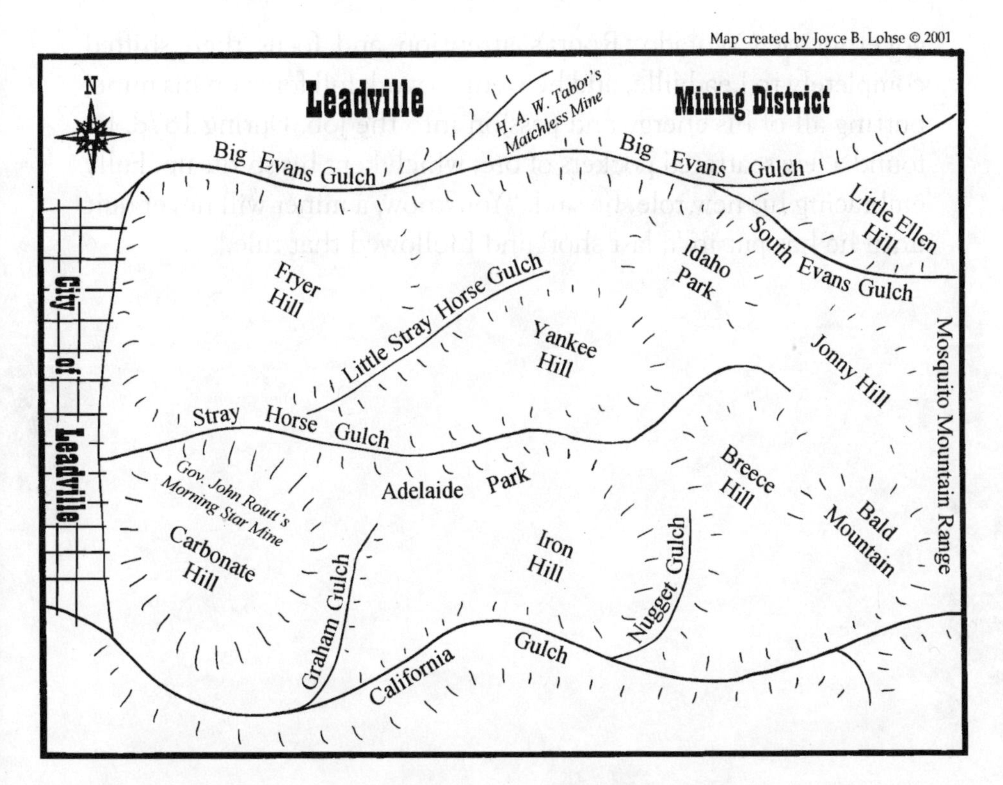

Leadville Mining Region. Routt's Morning Star Mine was located on Carbonate Hill adjacent to the town of Leadville.

build Denver up to its potential, Routt's term ran smoothly and satisfactorily, and the state's financial condition improved under his leadership.

Routt's prior experiences in public office in Illinois helped him deal effectively with taxes, budgets, and the school land board, which he oversaw as president. His supervision led to the successful development of a state school land system. All benefited from his good sense, loyalty to the state's welfare, and his relentless work ethic. Attention to his mining interests does not appear to have detracted from his effectiveness while acting as leader of the state, although writer Frank Hall observed sarcastically that Routt's efforts in Leadville, "were interrupted by occasional visits to the State Capitol until his term expired."[6]

With personal finances stretched to the limit, Routt declined to run for another term as governor. Frederick W. Pitkin was elected governor of Colorado. Routt's attention and focus then shifted completely to Leadville, and he went to work full force on his mine, putting all of his energy and passion into the job. During 1878, he found a few scattered pockets of ore, which kept his spirits up. Fully embracing his new role, he said, "You know, a miner will never quit until he has put in 'a last shot' and I followed that rule."[7]

ENDNOTES

Chapter 6—The Lure of Leadville

1. *Colorado State Business Directory and Annual Register* (Denver: J. A. Blake & Ives Publishers, 1878-85).

2. Don L. and Jean Harvey Griswold, *History of Leadville and Lake County, Colorado* (Denver: Colorado Historical Society, 1996), 145.

3. Ibid., 141, 145-146.

4. Richard D. Lamm, *Pioneers and Politicians*, (Boulder: Pruett Publishing, 1984), 30. See also, *Denver Times*, 26 March 1907.

5. Ibid.

6. Griswold, *History of Leadville and Lake County, Colorado*, 146.

7. Edward Blair, *Leadville, Colorado's Magic City* (Boulder: Pruett Publishing, 1980), 30.

Stereoscopic view of Morning Star Mine, Leadville, ca. 1880. *Courtesy Colorado Historical Society, 84-192.14.*

7
The Morning Star

"LILA! LILA! WE STRUCK IT RICH!" It is easy to imagine an excited John Routt bursting through the front door and shouting the good news to his patient wife. How proud he must have been on that day in mid-April 1879 when he returned from Leadville to Denver to tell Eliza of his success. The Morning Star Mine was going to make them rich. All the hard work and sacrifice had paid off, and John Routt was coming home. The *Rocky Mountain News*, April 16, 1879, declared simply, "Ex-Governor Routt has returned from Leadville."

During the remainder of the year, almost $300,000 of valuable silver ore was extracted from the Morning Star. By 1880, the mine was paying about $72,000 a month. In an understated comment, the *Rocky Mountain News*, April 26, 1879, described Routt's new role: "The ex-governor of the state, Hon. John L. Routt, having bonded his mines in Leadville, is beginning to be regarded as a *bonanza king*."

John Routt had officially entered the select fraternity known as Bonanza Kings, a title bestowed upon those who found great wealth in the mining camps. To his friends, he would say, "I hitched my wagon to a star and won. One day, we broke into the 'blanket' of ore and my troubles were over."[1]

When Routt bought the Morning Star, it was a twelve-foot hole in the ground on the side of Carbonate Hill. By the time his crew reached pay dirt, the Morning Star's main shaft reached 100 feet into the earth. It had a 200-foot drift, a 4-foot pay vein, 3-foot pitch, and a 20-by-30-foot shaft house.

In an effort to keep control of mineral transactions, several mine owners organized a Mining and Stock Exchange in Leadville. According to Leadville's newspaper, *The Eclipse*, quoted in the *Rocky Mountain News*, April 30, 1879, "The movement recently inaugurated looking to the establishment of a Mining and Stock exchange in our city, seems to be taking substantial form. A meeting for its furtherance was held at the Clarendon Hotel on Saturday evening, when about fifty names were enrolled as members." H.A.W. Tabor was president, and the organizing membership included John L. Routt.

Once the Morning Star began producing silver, the Routts were able to pay off their debts and invest in new enterprises. In August, John Routt became a director for another mining company, the Leadville National Mining and Milling Company. Built upon a capital stock of $1 million, it had branch offices in New York and Boston, with its headquarters in Leadville.

With money pouring in, John Routt began living the life of a Bonanza King in Denver. His first order of business was to present Eliza with $100,000, which she managed and maintained wisely, as he knew she would. He also bought her a fine Victorian mansion. It was an elegant residence at 327 Welton Street, on the corner Fourteenth Street, in the heart of Denver. The address was renumbered in 1887 and remained 1355 Welton thereafter.

Fourteenth Street was known as Governor's Row. Public officials and Bonanza Kings built fine mansions there, many exceeding the Routts' home in opulence. The dirt street composed of compacted sand and gravel was watered down frequently by the eighteen sprinkling wagons maintained by the city to keep the dust down from the traffic of elegant horse-drawn carriages. Sidewalks paved with diamond-shaped marble slabs lined the streets. In the twilight about an hour-and-a-half before dusk, residents paraded their carriages up and down Governor's Row, putting their fine horses and carriages on display. Tidy lawns were maintained with stunning flowering displays. Denver was booming.

The Routts' new home was purchased for $30,000 from C. B. Kountze and remained in the family as long as John and Eliza were living. The grounds were spacious, with a neatly maintained lawn and a garden full of beautiful blooming roses and other flowers. A tree grew in the yard from a twig transplanted from a walnut tree on the Hanks-Lincoln homestead, a reminder of the Routts' Illinois heritage and friendship with Lincoln.

A portrait of President Grant was prominently displayed as part of the eclectic Victorian décor of the beautiful home. Statuary and select samples of ore, marble, and granite from the mines were exhibited. Paintings by the Routt children adorned the walls. When John began raising cattle, he added a portrait of one of their finest imported cattle and a unique chair made of cattle horns.

The Routts' home at Fourteenth and Welton Streets was Colorado's first Governor's Mansion. *Denver Post*, August 13, 1907.

The Routts became part of Denver's lively social scene of families made rich by mining. Prominent in that scene was Routt's friend, Lieutenant Governor Horace Austin Warner Tabor, who was widely known as the Silver King of Leadville. Tabor's mining investments in Leadville, including the Matchless Mine, made him enormously wealthy. His annual investment income was estimated at $4 million a year, with $1 million of that coming from the Matchless Mine. He enjoyed spending his newly earned money with flare and abandon.

Although they were quite different in character, Tabor and Routt lived parallel lives and held many experiences in common. They often appeared together at political and business events, as well as social gatherings. Tabor's grandiose wealth and heavily documented personal life, is a well-known part of Colorado history. Artifacts from his life lend valuable clues about the lifestyle and experiences of Tabor and his contemporaries such as the Routts, as well as the manner in which the families handled their newfound wealth.

A newspaper account tells of an extravagant party given by Horace Tabor and his first wife, Augusta, for the prominent citizens of Denver in February 1879. John and Eliza Routt assisted the Tabors with the party and in receiving their guests that evening. For the occasion, Augusta Tabor, who preferred to downplay their wealth much of the time, wore an elegant gown of black silk and velvet trimmed with canary-colored silk and diamond ornaments. Eliza wore a dress of dark green silk and with a velvet train, also decorated with diamond ornaments. Newspapers of the time delighted in describing the minute details of these functions. On this occasion, they described the conversation, décor, entertainment, food, and drink as spectacular, lavish, and unforgettable.

Those days of gold and silver strikes were exciting ones in mining camps such as Leadville. However, many accidents, which were not uncommon, served as a grim reminder of the danger and sacrifice necessary to maintain the production of precious minerals from the mines. Tragedy visited the Morning Star Mine in August 1879. The *Rocky Mountain News* reported the following:

Killed in Routt's Mine

The *Eclipse* newspaper says) a man was instantly killed at the Morning Star mine, on Carbonate hill, by the caving in of dirt from the roof of a drift. The man was a German, and we did not learn his name. Later last evening, parties were down hunting for the coroner, but the inquest has been deferred till this morning. The body was taken to the man's home, but the inquest will probably be held at Rogers' undertaking rooms. The property in which the accident occurred belongs to Governor Routt and Joseph W. Watson.[2]

In April 1880, John Routt became president of the Morning Star Consolidated, which included seven separate mining claims on twenty-six acres in Leadville. The mines included in the company were the Morning Star, Waterloo, Halfway House, Forsaken, Buckeye Belle, Anchor, and Carrolton. His partners were Colorado State Treasurer George C. Corning and Joseph W. Watson, his manager at the Morning Star.

On March 14, 1880, the status of the Morning Star Mine was described in the *Daily News*.

The most productive mine yet worked on Carbonate Hill is the Morning Star and Waterloo consolidation. This the property of Governor Routt, J. W. Watson and George C. Corning, all three being now in New York, where a sale of the mine for three millions of dollars is now pending. The ore already mined from the property has amounted to over a million of dollars, and the underground workings have been conducted in a most systematic manner; pushing developments constantly ahead and exposing a great deal more mineral than has been taken out. The ore mined, in fact, has been mostly taken from development drifts and but little stoping has been done. The opening up and operating the mine has been under the personal supervision of Mr. Watson, who has had years of experience in mining and thoroughly understands its details. The timbering through the drifts and workings are particularly substantial and more attention has been paid to keeping the mine in good shape than to the surface improvements. The hoisting works, for instance, although good and substantial, are not extensive enough for so important a mine. To this fact is due the reason the shipments are not greater as the hoisting facilities are taxed to their utmost to raise the sixty or seventy tons of ore produced daily. The capabilities of the mine are far beyond this. At no time in the history of the mine has the property looked better than at present, or a greater amount of ore been mined. The extensive levels and drifts are being pushed forward as rapidly as can be, still opening out new and large bodies of ore, while the pillars of wealth left standing and already developed are left undisturbed for the future. The best of experts have made careful estimates of the amount of reserve already exposed in the mines, and in no case have any of these calculations been below three millions of dollars. During the month of February the shipments of ore amounted to 1,471 tons. During the first part of the month the shipments, owing to some delays were smaller than usual, while during the latter part, and so far in the present month, from sixty to seventy tons are daily handled. The recent purchase by the owner [Routt] of the Morning Star, of the Half Way House, Forsaken, Buckeye Bell and other claims located down the hill to the north, nearer to Stray Horse gulch, are also being actively worked. During last month, owing to timbering and repairing these mines, a great deal of ore could not be extracted. From both the new mines during February, there were shipped one hundred and thirty tons. The production at present averages twelve tons daily. Some very fine ore has been taken from the Half Way House. One lot of over four tons, shipped last week, netted $200 to the ton. These properties are being rapidly developed, and will soon add largely to the shipments.[3]

In 1880, Leadville mines produced 9 million ounces of silver as labor problems disrupted the mining community at Carbonate Camp. Miners became increasingly disgruntled about working twelve hours a day, six days a week, in unsafe and unhealthy conditions for three dollars a day. Owners might argue that they had worked for similar wages and under similar conditions when they started prospecting, but the boomtown economy meant workers had greater personal expenses. Rail service brought new supplies of cheap immigrant labor arrived daily, keeping wages down. The Knights of Labor had secretly organized The Miner's Cooperative Union in Leadville, and a strike was imminent.

The situation came to a head when the workers in Horace Tabor's mines went on strike, marched down the gulch into Leadville, collecting some 4,000 men along the way. Smelter workers walked off the job to support the miners, bringing the total to 10,000 strikers. Tension escalated with threats of violence.

In 1878, Governor Routt had issued a proclamation incorporating the town, which Leadville citizens voted unanimously to accept. Horace Tabor, who with his wife, Augusta, had operated a general store and grubstaked miners when they first settled in Leadville, became first mayor and postmaster.

By 1880, Horace Tabor was lieutenant governor under Governor Frederick R. Pitkin. Although he preferred to have the title "Governor" used with his name, Tabor was never governor of Colorado. He was, however, very much in charge in Leadville where he organized his own local militia to maintain law and order. He called his militia the Tabor Light Cavalry and named himself commander, mobilizing his militia to subdue the strikers and to round up troublemakers. He also commanded that law authorities order miners back to work. The situation was volatile.

Governor Pitkin overruled Tabor's authority and militia by sending in David J. Cook, major general of the state militia, to help diffuse the situation. A conference between the miner's union and the mine owners was organized, and the meeting resulted in a peaceful agreement. Individuals who had resorted to violence and intimidation were not re-employed. Miners returned to their jobs with the same wages and working conditions, although management voted in favor of adopting a general eight-hour workday, which would become the prevailing law in the mining camp. As a result of the need for intervention by the state government, as well as his action against the community of miners, Horace Tabor's credibility was severely damaged.

During the three-week-long strike, production in the Morning Star Mine was suspended. Mine manager, J. W. Watson, and assistant manager, R. C. Facer, were in Denver during the strike. When peace was restored, the *Daily News* on March 14, 1880, reported that over a hundred men were lined up, waiting to apply for jobs at the Morning Star, once the managers returned and mining operations were resumed.

On October 7, 1880, the *Rocky Mountain News*, reprinting an article from the *Leadville Herald*, reported that Morning Star Mine employees presented a fine flag measuring 17-by-30 feet to the Morning Star Company. The large American flag was unfurled and conspicuously displayed from a flag pole over the east shaft building of the Morning Star Mine, and could easily be seen from all parts of the city. It was also reported that the mineworkers had organized a "Boys in Blue" club.

Perhaps the flag represented a peace offering, and the club represented newly kindled pride and solidarity, because the miners settled back into their work routine at the Morning Star. Still more reforms in wages and working conditions were to come, but Leadville miners had taken the first step in making their problems known.

In 1880, the Routts' friends, Horace and Augusta Tabor, experienced a personal crisis. Horace Tabor spent more and more time enjoying life as the Silver King of Leadville, away from his stoic wife, Augusta, whom he had safely deposited in a large home in Denver. On his own in Leadville, Horace spent money with abandon, built a lavish opera house, and fell madly in love with a beautiful young woman. (Recall the saying adopted by many of the Bonanza Kings that it takes one woman to help earn the fortune and another to help spend it.)

Many discarded pioneer women found themselves alone and penniless in the mountains, or on the streets of Denver. When Tabor sought a divorce from Augusta, she knew better than to leave herself open to destitution and would not agree to a divorce. Horace continued his relationship with his new love, Elizabeth McCourt Doe, known locally as "Baby Doe." Augusta eventually relented and unwillingly granted him a divorce that provided her a lucrative financial settlement, and Tabor and Baby Doe were married in 1883.

With so many changes and disruptions in the wake of financial boom in a rapidly growing and prospering state, Eliza Routt maintained consistency and solidarity in her own marriage and in the Routt household and family. Even though the Routts' situation was similar in many ways to that of the Tabors, John and Eliza's relationship, family, and household, as well as their social and political position, remained on solid ground and consistently above reproach.

"Uncle Johnny" Routt had a reputation for a generous nature and nonpartisan entertaining, and he teetered on the brink of careless spending at times. Eliza's sensible domestic management helped to keep her exuberant husband's excesses in check without compromising their lifestyle as public figures. Guests, political and personal, were entertained often in the Routt home.

One newspaper account suggested that Johnny Routt enjoyed cutting loose with the boys. During the Republican Convention of 1880 in Leadville, the *Rocky Mountain News* reported, "Thus far the convention marched on in its proceedings without impediment. When the nomination for state auditor was reached, Governor Routt, who had been around the corner, came in 'feeling like a morning star'. He had not made proper allowances for altitude, or possibly in the midst of the enthusiasm his drinks had been mixed."[4]

This quotation is especially interesting in the use of the phrase, *feeling like a morning star,* as an apparent simile for a hangover. On any account, Routt was well known for sharing his hospitality, enjoying the camaraderie of his friends and associates, and on occasion singing and drinking with them.

Early in 1880, at the age of 41, Eliza Pickrell Routt became pregnant. This pregnancy produced the Routts' only child together. Their daughter, Lila Elkin Routt, was born on November 11, 1880, and was given her mother's nickname, Lila, as her first name. Lila became the new center of the Routts' busy household and would grow up to become a favorite of Denver society. Educated in music, she would carry on her mother's interest in music appreciation through development and support of the Denver symphony and with her perfect soprano voice as a vocal soloist.

A little over a month after Lila's birth, on December 21, 1880, Eliza's "Grand Pa Pa," William F. Elkin, passed away in Decatur, Illinois. At age 86, his long and productive life of public service in Illinois had come to an end. Eliza's grandfather had filled the role of her father throughout her life. An important link to Eliza's family was gone.

ENDNOTES

Chapter 7—The Morning Star

1. Albert B. Sanford, "John L. Routt, First State Governor of Colorado," *Colorado Magazine* (August 1926): 84. Albert Sanford, who later became curator of the Colorado Historical Society, was personally acquainted with John Routt in Leadville.
2. *Rocky Mountain News*, 2 August 1879.
3. *Daily News*, 14 March 1880, 6.
4. *Rocky Mountain News*, 27 August 1880.

John L. Routt, ca. 1885, during his term as mayor of Denver. *Courtesy Colorado Historical Society*, #10026998.

8
The Bonanza King

DURING THE EARLY 1880S, John Routt settled into life as a Denver public figure, ex-governor, and Bonanza King. He continued to reinvest much of his revenue from the Morning Star into additional mines, stone quarries, ranch land, livestock, and his new home, and he contributed to many charitable causes. For recreation, John and Eliza joined an archery club, allowing them to enjoy together the latest craze in Victorian Denver.

Routt and his family indulged in a few well-chosen personal luxuries with their income from the Morning Star. In addition to the mansion and the money John had presented to Eliza, they purchased a beautiful carriage with a pair of finely matched horses at a cost of about $3,000, more than the value of John Routt's first home and property in Illinois.

There is no evidence that Routt was overcome with self-importance. The 1880 *Denver City Directory* listed Routt's occupation simply as "miner." The address of their home at that time was listed as 327 Welton Street. The 1880 Denver City census indicated a busy household at the Routt home. Occupants of the house were John Routt (53), ex-governor of Colorado; Lila [Eliza, with two years subtracted] (39); Minnie J. (13); Birdie M. (12); Francis Bruce (33), Routt's coachman from Maryland; his wife Ellen Bruce (32), servant; Emma Peterson (25), servant from Sweden; Jennie Stull (25), governess from Illinois; and Hathaway Jones (21), Eliza's cousin, listed as a visitor from Illinois.

The Routts' neighbors on Welton Street, according to the census, were Dr. Hamilton Riddle (36), his wife Francis (32), and their four children. Hamilton "Rush" Riddle was Eliza's half brother, born to her mother and her second husband, Abner Riddle, shortly before her mother died. Although Rush Riddle and his family eventually returned to Illinois, Eliza managed to keep close ties with her family and had many visitors from Illinois over the years, just as John had promised they would in his early letters to her during their whirlwind courtship.

In 1880, John Routt attended the Republican National Convention in Chicago to lend support to his former general and personal friend, Ulysses S. Grant, who was seeking his third nomination to the presidency. Routt was one of a coalition of "306 Grant Men" who stood in solid support of Grant. However, Grant lost the nomination to Senator-elect James A. Garfield of Ohio. When he learned he would not run for a third term, Grant said, "I feel a great responsibility lifted from my shoulders." Routt remained a staunch and loyal supporter, ignoring Grant's critics and proclaiming Grant the greatest man this country has produced.[1]

Following this political defeat, Grant's travels led him to Colorado for a tour and a visit with his good friend John Routt, who acted as his personal host and guide. Responding to a longstanding invitation from the Union Veteran's Association of Leadville and the Denver and Rio Grande Railroad, Grant visited the mining community of Leadville.

Grant and his contingency arrived by train at Leadville on the evening of July 23, 1880, as guests of the Tabor Opera House management. Amid a raucous, cheering crowd of some 30,000 revelers, Grant was conveyed down Harrison Street, Leadville's main street, in a carriage pulled by four black horses whose backs had been sprinkled with gold dust. The route into town was lined with over 100 bonfires lighting the cloudy evening sky. Arches over the street made of flags and pine boughs framed printed slogans such as "Welcome President" and "True To Liberty." A special banquet was arranged at the Clarendon Hotel, the likes of which had never been seen before, in or near the mining camp. Champagne flowed throughout the sumptuous feast of beef tenderloin and speckled trout. As spirits were poured liberally and tongues loosened, speeches in praise of the former president extended well into the night. Horace Tabor had masterminded the arrival festivities and was master of ceremonies.

When it was his turn to address the gathering, ex-Governor Routt delivered a speech entitled, "The Mining Interests of the Country." Realizing that those preceding him at the podium had already exhausted the subject, Routt kept his remarks light and humorous. This strategy recaptured the audience's attention so that he was able to convey his main point, which was to encourage respect for the mining profession.

During his stay in Leadville, Grant was escorted on a tour of the mining district. When asked if he wished to descend into Routt's Morning Star Mine, the "grizzled warrior" declined, stating that he didn't much like the looks of the buckets, the main conveyance vehicle for descending into the shaft. Instead, Grant visited the Iron Mine for his underground tour.

Grant, his wife, and Routt attended two plays—*Our Boarding House* and *Ours*—at the Tabor Opera House. When the party left Leadville after the five-day visit, the delegation continued on by railroad to Cañon City, Colorado Springs, and Manitou Springs, before returning to Denver. Grant and Routt left the train at South Arkansas.

As planned, Routt and Grant embarked on a two-week camping trip, to inspect Colorado's mining country and to relax. With no set schedule, the men rode by horseback and in a spring wagon pulled by a team of mountain ponies through Salida, the San Luis Valley over Poncha Pass, to Gunnison, Almont, Ruby, Pitkin, and Aspen, visiting mining camps throughout the mountains before returning to Denver.

One night, the travelers stopped at an isolated cabin and asked its proprietor for shelter for the night. Their host was a Union Army veteran. How surprised he was to find not only Governor Routt at his doorstep, but also ex-President Ulysses S. Grant. The befuddled man insisted on digging out a picture of Grant to compare with the man who had appeared at his cabin door, to make sure it really was the general.

During an overnight stay in one cabin, the bed they were forced to share collapsed, dumping the ex-president and ex-governor unceremoniously onto the floor. This provided a great episode for jokes and stories they told later about their mountain adventure. Routt would end the story by saying, "What a fall there was, my countrymen!"[2]

Once the travelers returned to Denver, Grant was treated to several excursions and daytrips into the mountains. One wagon ride took him up to the mining town of Idaho Springs, then up to Blackhawk. On the return trip to Idaho Springs, Routt decided to play a little trick on Grant, who enjoyed a good, fast wagon ride with spirited horses. Without Grant's knowledge, Routt asked the wagon driver to give them a lively ride home at full speed. Jehu Bill Mullins did just that.

They charged down Virginia Canyon toward Idaho Springs with the team of horses thundering dangerously around blind curves at breakneck speed. The wagon lurched and rolled, first tipping to one side, then shifting to the other side, shaking, rattling, careening around sharp turns, as the horses raced wildly down the rough mountain road. At the end of the wild ride, Grant leapt from the wagon, approached the driver, and handed him $50, saying, "Such an experience is worth more than I can afford to pay, so take this as a souvenir of our trip."[3]

Wherever he went throughout the state, Grant was greeted by crowds of well-wishers and curiosity seekers, straining to get a glimpse of the nation's most celebrated war hero. On August 16, Grant's entourage went by train to Colorado Springs and Manitou Springs. Upon their return to Denver, Grant was greeted by crowds and a prancing gray horse, which he rode in a parade and procession through Denver streets, viewing decorations of flowers and bunting, pausing in front of the Routt home to admire its bounteous floral decor.

When they reached the Glenarm Hotel, a block from the Routt home, there was much cheering from the crowds and shouts of

"Grant!" "Grant!" and "Speech!" "Speech!" By this time, Grant was tired. Stepping out onto his balcony, Grant addressed the crowd. He said, "Ladies and Gentleman: I will present to you Governor Routt, who, I have heard, has been making speeches all over the state. He is fond of speaking."

The amiable crowd responded by shouting, "Routt!" "Routt!"

Grant's friend came to the rescue. John Routt stepped forward and said, "I appreciate the compliment, ladies and gentlemen, but the General has been telling yarns about me; if you will wait until tomorrow night, or until the next day night [*sic*], you will hear General Grant speak, he will then be in good trim."[4]

Routt's diplomacy and ability to create order from chaos came in handy once again. The crowd quietly dispersed, clearing the streets, and Grant was left alone to take his rest.

In September 1881, John Routt sold the Morning Star Mine. He closed the sale in New York City for a reported $1.5 million. Later reports set the figure at $1 million. This amount was not quite up to the inflated value of $3 million, which had been published in the *Rocky Mountain News* eighteen months earlier before the price of silver began sliding downward. Still, $1 million was a huge sum in 1881, even after all the bills and loans were paid. Who would have thought, including Routt himself, that after only six years in the state, John Routt would become a Bonanza King?

Despite Johnny Routt's occasional wild and rowdy impulses, indulgence in hard drink, and frequent use of earthy language, he was a member and staunch supporter of the church, perhaps due to Eliza's influence and encouragement. They arrived in Denver bearing a letter of recommendation from her church in Illinois, and were welcomed as members of the newly formed Central Christian Church.

The church had no building of its own and met in many facilities, including tents. In 1882, the Reverend William Bayard Craig was coaxed into coming to Denver to act as minister of the church. While in Denver, Craig became a well-known charismatic minister and church leader. The town of Craig in Moffat County in the northwest corner of Colorado was named in his honor.

Within a year of Craig's arrival, a property on Broadway between Sixteenth and Seventeenth Streets was purchased to build a church. This real estate transaction was made possible by a generous gift of $10,000 from John and Eliza, which was followed with other donations to help finance the purchase of the property.

John Routt continued his political activities and business endeavors. After baby Lila's birth, the *Rocky Mountain News* noted that the cultured presence of Mrs. Routt was missing from social circles due to ill health and the care of her "interesting young family."[5] It was, however, during this time that she enthusiastically joined in the effort to establish the Orphan's Home Association as a member of its first Board of Managers elected in January 1881.

By 1883, John Routt had been working in the private sector for four years. His successor as governor, Frederick W. Pitkin, was at the end of his term, and James B. Grant was poised to begin his term. Routt's holdings, investments, and family occupied much of his time. His political aspiration during this time was to be elected senator. Although that position eluded him, he was elected to a two-year term as Denver's mayor when another candidate for the mayor's office was unable to accept the nomination. As was his habit, he not only accepted the call to public service, he threw himself into the job with dedication and energy.

A highlight of Routt's tenure as mayor came in July 1883. The city of Denver hosted a grand Mining Exposition to extol the virtues of rich and rare native minerals. Denver citizens crowded the streets where they were treated to a parade through Denver's downtown, from Larimer to Broadway, that featured bands, businesses, and celebrities such as Mayor Routt and Eliza, Governor James B. Grant, and ex-Senator Horace Tabor. The procession made its way to a newly constructed exhibition hall, where citizens could study displays of minerals used for industrial purposes as well as jewelry and adornment. At the opening ceremonies, Routt and Tabor took turns introducing speakers. As the representative of the city, Mayor Routt was called upon to speak after Governor James B. Grant.

> Not eighteen months ago, less than a dozen citizens of
> Denver originated the idea of starting an exposition and

> constructing a building for exposition purposes. They expected at the time to confine it only to the State of Colorado, but the people of the state and the people of adjoining states responded so magnificently that these gentlemen conceived the new idea of giving the Exposition a new name and christening it "The National Mining and Industrial Exposition". We of Denver feel especially interested in the success of this enterprise. ... I trust that all our visiting friends may be benefited by what they see here today.[6]

In 1885, when his term as mayor ended, John Routt ran for the U.S. Senate, a position he fervently wanted. At the time, senatorial candidates were selected by state legislators rather than public election. Routt's widespread popularity and reputation for honesty were on his side, but his opponents had the advantage of greater wealth and power.

The race for the Republican nomination was close between Routt and Nathaniel Hill, a political opponent whom he despised on ethical grounds. The balance was upset when a dark-horse candidate, Henry M. Teller, split the vote and siphoned off Routt supporters. Hill's disdain for Teller was even greater than his contempt for Routt.

Hill sent a messenger to Routt proposing that he and Routt combine efforts to defeat Teller. The messenger found Routt brooding, lying face down on a bed in party headquarter at the Windsor Hotel in Denver. Routt's response was to raise up on one elbow and say, "Otto, you remind me of just such ________ who took a man up into a high place and offered him all of the surrounding country if he would cast his lot with him. And, Otto, don't you know the ________ didn't own an inch of that country?" The offer was thus soundly rejected.

When Teller heard about Hill's offer and Routt's rejection, Teller went to visit Routt and found him still prone and listless. He said, "Now, John, the thing for you to do is to call back your men and I will withdraw in your favor, and with the Hillites with you, you can be selected on the first ballot."

Routt sat up and stared at Teller. Then he replied, "Not by a ________, Teller; they hate you worse than they do me; you have got to stick and they will get a dose of their own medicine."[7]

Routt lost the Republican Party's nomination by only four votes. Teller won the nomination, and Routt lost his only chance to become a senator. That hotly contested senate race caused residual debate, friction, and bad feelings for many years among Colorado politicians. Over the years, Nathaniel Hill's presence on the political scene continued to antagonize Routt. The situation was not improved when Hill built a sprawling, lavish mansion diagonally across the street from the Routts.

During the same year, Routt lost his longtime friend, Ulysses S. Grant, who died of throat cancer on July 23, 1885. On the advice of his son, Grant had invested what money he had in an unsuccessful banking venture. By the time he died, he was completely broke. Days before his death, he finished writing his memoirs. Later published by Mark Twain, the earnings from the book became a large part of Grant's estate.

In a quiet and kindly manner, John Routt came to the aid of his friend one last time. A handwritten receipt signed by a secretary, M. S. Noah, simply states: "Denver July 28/85 – Recd. of Gov. J. L. Routt amount subscribed in order to defray Expenses to Genl. Grant's Funeral."[8]

Denver July 28/85
Recd of Gov J. L. Routt
amount Subscribed in order
to defray Expenses to Genl Grants
Funeral
M. S. Noah
Fin Secy

On October 29, 1885, there was happier news from Sangamon County, Illinois, when Eliza's 36-year-old cousin Emma Pickrell married the Reverend William Bayard Craig. Emma's father was Eliza's uncle, William Pickrell, a pious man who conducted religious services in Sangamon County and tended to the spiritual needs of the community with the assistance of his daughter, "Miss Emma." Experience and background made Emma well suited to the life of a minister's wife.

After her marriage to Reverend Craig, Emma came to live in Denver as wife of the popular minister. She and Eliza became inseparable friends and remained close for the rest of their lives.

In the meantime, the Routts' daughter Lila commanded much of their time and attention at home. In an especially extravagant display to encourage appreciation of the arts, the Routts commissioned a statue of their daughter to be sculpted from Italian marble. On February 25, 1886, the statue was formally unveiled during an elegant evening of celebration and socializing, during which music was played and poetry was read. Little Lila, a six-year-old at the time, unveiled the statue, which portrayed her as a three-year-old.

Reverend Craig delivered an address about the beauty and importance of childhood and of art in the home. Eliza and John, the proud parents, were congratulated, and after several musical numbers, popular local author Mrs. Patience Stapleton read a poem she had written for the occasion.

The evening was reported as a grand success enhanced by classical music and distinguished guests. After an address by Reverend Craig entitled, "The Child in the Midst," little Lila unveiled the marble statue of her likeness to the delight of the gathered guests.

Reverend Craig must have been especially touched by the whole affair considering he was about to become a father himself. Emma gave birth to a little boy in November, whom they named Bayard Pickrell Craig. Sadly, the little boy, their only child, did not live four years.

The 1886 Christmas issue of *Harper's Weekly* magazine included a large double-page Christmas sketch by artist Thomas Nast, inspired by the marble statue of Lila Routt during a visit by Nast to the Routt home. The sketch showed Lila hanging stockings by the chimney, with the caption, "Santa Claus can't say that I've forgotten anything."[10]

Lila's Statue

In olden times a stork went winging
With quiet babes close to its downy breast;
So in this day a ship came, bringing
A little maiden out to the West.

A tiny marble maid, as if the snow
Of the far frozen North had caught her fast,
Like the ice maid we read of long ago,
Who loved the sun that melted her at last.

But this white child has a sister sweet
A rosy double all witchery and grace
The house echoes the patter of her feet
Neath meadow ponds in a colder clime.

There is naught in sculptured stone so fine,
Hero or heroine or virgin mild,
As this—most human, most divine—
A little, innocent, happy child.

In shady churchyards by noonday light,
Where winds are bitter cold, or softly blow—
In night's gloomy derth or pale moonlight
Marble cherubs watch sleeping babes below.

In dainty rooms that child of stone will stand
While her rosy model grows to womanhood;
May Lila's life like it be pure and grand—
A triumph of all that is true and good.[9]

Thomas Nast used Lila Routt's likeness from a marble statue as a model for this Christmas illustration published in *Harper's Weekly*, December 1886.

Another sketch by Nast appeared on the cover of the January 8, 1887 *Harper's Bazar* magazine two weeks later, featuring baby Elizabeth Pearl "Lillie" Tabor. She was the daughter of Routt's contemporary, Horace Tabor, and his second wife, Elizabeth "Baby Doe" Tabor.

Having art featuring their children on the cover of national magazines was only one demonstration of the life of wealth, prestige, and elegance enjoyed by the Bonanza Kings of Denver in the late nineteenth century.

ENDNOTES

Chapter 8—The Bonanza King

1. *Daily News*, 13 August 1907, 2.
2. *Magazine of Western History* 9, no. 4 (February 1889): 458.
3. *Denver Times*, 12 October 1899.
4. *Rocky Mountain News*, 17 August 1880, 8.
5. *Rocky Mountain News*, 20 February 1881, 2.
6. *Daily News*, 18 July 1883.
7. *Daily News*, 13 August 1907.
8. Colorado State Archives, file #9353.
9. *Daily News*, 26 February 1886.
10. *Harper's Weekly* 30, no.15 (December 25, 1886): 66.

Cache la Poudre River Canyon. Irrigation ditches brought water from the river to the Routt's ranch near the canyon. *Photographer: Joyce Lohse*.

Back at the Ranch

EARLY IN 1884, John L. Routt and his sons, Frank and John H., began purchasing parcels of ranch land north of Fort Collins. According to the February issue of the *Colorado Livestock Record* that year, "Ex-Governor Routt has purchased the Meldrum Ranch near Fort Collins and the ranch is one of the most valuable in the State … the price paid was a liberal one."[1]

The ranch land was located between Fort Collins and Livermore, in the Livermore Valley. It is a region of beautiful bluffs, fields, and canyons adjoining the banks of the Cache la Poudre River, north of Laporte, in an area called Pleasant Valley. Routt named his 5,000-acre ranch Marble Glen. The picturesque grazing land was at the south end of a rocky canyon. In the not-too-distant past, fur trappers, traders, and Native Americans had camped on the ridge overlooking the valley.

In the Larimer County Courthouse in Fort Collins, deeds show that in 1884 and 1885, John Routt and his sons bought parcels of land in close proximity to one another. Some deeds for the Routt ranches specifically state that water rights were included. N. H. Meldrum, ex-secretary of state, had owned the largest portion of the land, which was part of a larger spread called Kremer's Ranch before Meldrum owned it.

General Index Grantee—Book No. 3 in the Larimer County Courthouse in Fort Collins shows the following Routt land purchases in 1884 and 1885:

1/15/84— John L. Routt from Elmore Vanderwark, A. C. Gordon, George W. Meldrum
9/8/84— Frank C. Routt from Joshua & H. W. Budd
9/17/84— Frank C. Routt from Charles C. Creed, Jno. G. Creed & wife
10/31/84— John H. Routt from Chas. M. Cranson
11/10/84— John H. Routt from Chas. E. Black
11/10/84— Frank C. Routt from Chas. H. Marsh
11/15/84— Frank C. Routt from John Carrell
12/8/84— John H. Routt from Daniel Cameron
12/15/84— Frank C. Routt from Hugh McBride
12/30/84— Frank C. Routt from William B. Woodruff
2/9/85— Frank C. Routt from Owen T. Gebhart
6/9/85— Frank C. Routt from E. B. Runyan
6/24/85— John L. Routt from Greeley Salt Lake and Pacific Railroad Company
8/10/85— Franklin [sic] C. Routt from John L. Routt
11/13/85— John L. Routt from John H. Routt

Ex-governor Routt used his ranch to raise cattle and crops through irrigation. Although not as lucrative as his mining enterprises, cattle ranching became a passion that would occupy him for many years. The ranch also provided a welcome retreat from the bustling city life, social obligations, mayoral duties, and his position on the Board of Capitol Managers, a committee formed to supervise the design and construction of the new state capitol building. He delighted in riding for miles on horseback showing his spread to visitors.

Although there is no record of Eliza visiting the ranch, she might have enjoyed visiting there and being outdoors as much as John. Perhaps she spent time in the orchard and garden with her young daughter, or rode horseback with her husband to inspect livestock and fences.

When a reporter from the *Fort Collins Courier* visited John Routt on the ranch in the summer of 1885, he observed:

> The governor was found at home in his working clothes and doing as much work as any man on his ranch. So rapidly has work been prosecuted and improvements made on the ranch that it has outgrown all expectations, and this can be more readily appreciated when it is known that the governor since going on his ranch has expended $40,000 in improvements. The high line ditch, from which water is taken to irrigate the ranch, is a wonder of engineering skill, and the difficulties which the proposed scheme presented, to begin with, would have disheartened any other man than the sturdy old governor. For three miles west, from the mouth of the Poudre canon the ditch is made, sometimes in soil, sometimes through solid rock, and there are nearly two miles of flume hung onto the sides of great rocks, fastened here and there by blockings of stone or by timbers and spieling. This mountain ditch is a wonderful sight not only on account of its novelty, but for the substantial nature of the improvement. Water gauges are well constructed, and there is not the least danger of flooding or any of the evils caused by defective headgates.
>
> Governor Routt's ranch property comprises, at present, 3,000 acres, all under a superb four and five-wire fence. Good fencing is a hobby with the governor. Besides having good posts, well set, he has given an additional strength and permanency to his fences by using heavy wire braces, which hold the fence wires rigidly in a certain place, making it impossible to move one part of the fence without taking it all.[2]

The report described 200 acres of alfalfa as coming up nicely. The governor was quoted as saying, "It has the best soil in the world in which to grow," referring to the loamy soil near the Cache la Poudre River. Other crops included corn, oats, and root crops to feed livestock, as well as a garden and orchard, creating what the reporter described as a "model farm." By soon adding 6,000 acres to his spread, he would have one of the largest stock farms in Colorado.

Routt's exceptional management skills were once again reflected in the success of his ranching enterprise. His only disaster came in the early days of the ranch. Routt's herd was started from cattle brought in from the warmer climate of Kentucky. The stock had some difficulty adapting to the harshness of winter on the Colorado range, and there were some winter losses. The herd eventually adapted and flourished. Routt experimented with crossing Durham with his Polled Angus cattle and produced a sleek, black-coated, hardy Angus breed.

Routt's cattle were marked with his historic registered "306" brand. He chose this brand to represent the delegation of 306 Grant men, of which he was a loyal member, during the thirty-six nomination votes cast for president at the 1880 Republican National Convention in Chicago. Routt further established his identity as a serious cattleman when he presided over three inter-state cattle conventions, earning himself yet another title, *Cattle King*.

In November 1884, John Routt was honored at the National Cattle and Horse Grower's Association Convention in St. Louis, Missouri. In gratitude for his past service to the association, Routt was presented with a chair made of burnished cow horns, which he had used while he presided over the association. The chair became a prized decoration in his home in Denver. When called upon to speak to the convention, Routt said:

> I have nothing special to say, except to thank the convention for their kind support. No man ever occupied a chair in this country whose effort to keep order was more kindly endorsed and seconded by a convention than was mine. I have looked over your faces so many times that they are very familiar to me—they are very strong ones; good faces, with character marks sticking out everywhere. You are good men; strong men; and I feel very grateful to you for the manner in which you have treated me as your presiding officer. You have been so kind; you have been so considerate, that it gives me a great deal of pleasure to hope that we will come together some other time, and look into each other's faces again. Some of this delegation will probably not be

> here, but it is to be hoped that all, each member of the convention, will come together again. It does us good to compare notes and look each other in the face.[3]

His sentimental response to the presentation of the chair was:

> Gentlemen, I thank you for this testimonial. It is worth to me more than some article that would cost ten thousand dollars. I will take this home and save it to remember you by. Every time I see these horns my thoughts will be called back to this National Convention of ours. There are many things connected with the deliberations of this Convention that will remain green in my memory all the way through the balance of the short time that I have to remain on this terrestrial globe. I am older than a great many of you—pretty strong, pretty vigorous, physically; but I am fifty-seven years of age. I appreciate this gift, gentlemen, very much. I broke it in—almost wore it out—and I am entitled to it for the balance of my days.[4]

Although Routt's ranch was not his most lucrative enterprise, especially compared with the Morning Star Mine, he enjoyed ranching and sharing the enterprise with his sons. He became more deeply involved when he joined efforts to create a Cattle Growers' Stockyard on the Mississippi or Missouri River so that he and his fellow cattlemen could better protect their interests in livestock transactions.

When Routt went to Denver to attend to his political commitments, such as the Board of Capitol Managers, his direct approach to problem solving was often called upon. One incident involved his oldest son, Frank. Frank had drilled a tunnel a mile-and-a-half long through a hill to connect an irrigation ditch and flume to transport water to his ranch. According to a retrospective piece printed in the *Denver Times* on October 12, 1899, ranchers in the area decided that Frank was getting more than his share of water from the canal. As a result, they tore down the flume he had built to transport water. When Frank appeared on the scene during the destruction, he pulled a gun on the intruding ranchers and said in a most direct way, "If you touch that flume again, now or at any other time, I will kill you, every one of you!"

The shaken ranchers went directly to Fort Collins to dispatch a frantic telegram to Frank's father, telling him about the trouble. Routt immediately boarded a train to Fort Collins.

The excited ranchers met Routt at the train station and repeated their story, telling him how Frank had threatened to kill them.

John Routt asked, "What for?"

The ranchers answered, "On account of his ditch. He says he will kill every one of us if we touch his ditch again."

Routt said, "Why, did Frank say that?"

"Yes, he did. He said it, every word."

Pondering this for a moment, John Routt said, "Well, by _____, if Frank said he would kill you, he will do it—*Watch out*!" With that, he walked away from the astonished group and returned to Denver.[5]

This story provides an amusing insight into the personality of the ex-Governor and his son and into the times in which they lived. The story also demonstrates the seriousness of water rights and irrigation. Because of the semiarid climate, agriculturalists in Colorado spend much of their money, time, and energy to transport water to crops and livestock. Interruption of the flow caused threats of gunfire many times in the history of the state.

The Routt sons moved to Pleasant Valley in late 1884, while they were still accumulating ranch land. In June 1885, the home of Routt's son, John, and most of its contents, was destroyed by fire. John was working in the field at the time. His wife and a hired girl worked desperately to put out the fire, but were able to save only a few belongings. A valuable hunting gun was listed among the losses. There was only a small amount of insurance on the structure. John's wife, Annie, moved in with Denver relatives while a new house was built.

Seven months later, during the winter night of January 22, 1886, Frank Routt's house on railroad land at the mouth of the Poudre Canyon burned to the ground and was declared a total loss. Frank was just able to rouse his wife and children and to retrieve some valuable papers before the house and all of their belongings burned.

229

(1044.) No 16155 WARRANTY DEED.—Colorado.—Culver, Page, Hoyne & Co., Stationers, 118 and 120 Monroe Street, Chicago.

This Deed, Made this twenty Ninth day of January in the year of our Lord one thousand eight hundred and eighty four between George W. Meldrum of the County of Larimer and State of Colorado, of the first part, and John L. Routt of the County of Arapahoe and State of Colorado, of the second part:

WITNESSETH, that the said party of the first part, for and in consideration of the sum of Six thousand and one hundred (6,100) 00/100 Dollars, to the said party of the first part in hand paid by the said party of the second part, the receipt whereof is hereby confessed and acknowledged, hath granted, bargained, sold and conveyed, and by these presents doth grant, bargain, sell, convey and confirm unto the said party of the second part, his heirs and assigns, forever, all the following described lots or parcels of land, situate, lying and being in the County of Larimer and State of Colorado, to wit:

The North East quarter (NE¼) of the South East quarter (¼) of Section Eleven (11) and the North half (N½) of the South West quarter (SW¼) and the North West quarter (NW¼) of the South East quarter (SE¼) of Section twelve (12). Also the South East quarter (SE¼) of the South East quarter (SE¼) of Section Eleven (11). And all of the East half of the North East quarter (NE¼) of Section fourteen (14). and so much of the North East quarter of the (SE¼) South East quarter of said Section fourteen (14) as lies on the North (N) and East (E) side of the Cache la Poudre River and so much of the South East quarter (SE¼) of the South East quarter (SE¼) of said Section fourteen (14) as lies on the North and East side of the said Cache la Poudre River. All of said lands being in Township Eight (8) North of Range Seventy (70) west. Containing about 320 acres more or less. Also all the right and interest of the party of the first part to the Canon Canal Company to supply said land with water.

TOGETHER with all and singular the hereditaments and appurtenances thereunto belonging or in anywise appertaining, and the reversion and reversions, remainder and remainders, rents, issues and profits thereof; and all the estate, right, title, interest, claim and demand whatsoever, of the said party of the first part, either in law or equity, of, in and to the above bargained premises, with the hereditaments and appurtenances: TO HAVE AND TO HOLD the said premises above bargained and described, with the appurtenances, unto the said party of the second part, his heirs and assigns forever. And the said George W. Meldrum party of the first part, for himself & his heirs, executors and administrators, doth covenant, grant, bargain and agree, to and with the said party of the second part, his heirs and assigns, that at the time of the ensealing and delivery of these presents, he was well seized of the premises above conveyed, as of good, sure, perfect, absolute and indefeasible estate of inheritance, in law, in fee simple, and hath good right, full power and lawful authority to grant, bargain, sell and convey the same, in manner and form aforesaid, and that the same are free and clear from all former and other grants, bargains, sales, liens, taxes, assessments and incumbrances of whatever kind or nature soever [excepting a Trust Deed for Eight Hundred and fifty dollars on SE¼ of SE¼ Sec 11 and E½ NE¼ and NE¼ SE¼ Sec 14] and the above bargained premises in the quiet and peaceable possession of the said party of the second part, his heirs and assigns, against all and every person or persons lawfully claiming or to claim the whole or any part thereof, the said party of the first part shall and will WARRANT AND FOREVER DEFEND.

IN WITNESS WHEREOF, the said party of the first part hath hereunto set his hand and seal the day and year first above written.

Signed, Sealed and Delivered in Presence of
The words "Excepting a Trust Deed for Eight Hundred & fifty dollars on the SE¼ of SE¼ of Sec 11 and E½ of NE¼ and NE¼ of SE¼ of Sec 14" interlined before signing.
Allen Steck

George W. Meldrum (SEAL)
(SEAL)
(SEAL)
(SEAL)

STATE OF COLORADO,
County of Arapahoe } ss. I, James S. Hudson a Notary Public in and for said County, in the State aforesaid, do hereby certify that George W. Meldrum personally known to me as the person whose name is subscribed to the annexed deed, appeared before me this day in person, and acknowledged that he signed, sealed and delivered the said instrument of writing as his free and voluntary act for the uses and purposes therein set forth.

James S. Hudson Notary Public. Arapahoe Co. Colorado

Given under my hand Notarial seal, this twenty Ninth day of January A. D. 1884

James S. Hudson
Notary Public.

Deed for the Meldrum property, dated January 29, 1884. The purchase was the beginning of Routt's acquisition of ranch land in Pleasant Valley.

Fires were not uncommon at the time, due to the prevalence of wood building materials and wood-burning stoves and fireplaces. However, it was reported that in the case of the fire at Frank's house, "The fire originated in a room where there was no fire, or anything that would be likely to cause a fire, and the origin of the conflagration is a mystery."[6]

Many years later in August 1898, a fire at Governor Routt's ranch destroyed an old barn originally erected by N. H. Meldrum, which was a landmark in the area. Harness and farm machinery valued at about $2,000 were lost and were only partially covered by insurance. A caretaker, B. M. Lasley, who was working in the basement of the barn at the time, was able to save five horses, although he suffered burns on his face and hands for his efforts.

After the turn of the century, Frank continued to manage the ranch. Although Eliza attended State Board of Agriculture meetings in Fort Collins until her resignation in 1905, John and Eliza never resided there. City directories, social yearbooks, and census records show their residence as Denver during all their years in Colorado.

ENDNOTES

Chapter 9—Back at the Ranch

1. *Colorado Livestock Record*, 1 February 1889, 5.
2. *Fort Collins Courier*, 4 June 1885, 8.
3. *Proceedings National Convention of Cattlemen*, St. Louis, Missouri (November 22, 1884): 10-11.
4. Ibid.
5. *Denver Times*, 12 October 1899.
6. *Fort Collins Weekly Express*, 30 January 1886, 1.

Eliza Routt, ca. 1890. The gown is likely the one she wore for John Routt's third-term inauguration. *Courtesy Colorado Historical Society*, *F-20.850*. (Image altered.)

10

Eliza Makes a Difference

ELIZA ROUTT CHANNELED her intelligence and energy into many worthy causes to improve her community and was a leader in the fight for equal rights for women. She and John wasted no time in joining the Central Christian Church in Denver where they generously contributed time and money to help it grow and evolve, and worked diligently in support of its charities. Their financial contributions helped the church move into a building of its own. The Routts also participated in gatherings outside of worship that included literary study groups and general socializing. They remained active members of the Central Christian Church throughout their life in Denver.

In 1877, Eliza Routt became a founding member of the Woman's Home Club. This organization provided safe and suitable housing for young working women in Denver. When this club later became a branch of the Young Women's Christian Association (YWCA), Eliza helped find a building for it. In 1899, the YWCA moved into a building at the corner of Sherman and Eighteenth Streets in downtown Denver.

Another of Eliza's early civic involvements was with the Denver Orphan's Home. The brick house was built in 1876 at 800 Logan Street in Denver. When the Denver Orphan's Home Association was established in 1881 to provide care and education for destitute, orphaned children, Eliza was elected to the board of directors. Eliza was motivated to help Denver's orphans. As an orphan herself, she empathized with the plight of children without parents. The Denver Orphan's Home Association was created by a group of twenty-one prominent citizens that included Elizabeth Byers and Margaret Gray Evans during a meeting of the Ladies Relief Society held in the home of Mrs. Evans, the organization's president. Dues for voting membership in the organization were set at five dollars per year, or one hundred dollars for a lifetime membership.

The Ladies Relief Society had its hands full giving groceries and coal for fuel to needy families, maintaining an old ladies' home, burying paupers, running a wood yard to give work to the unemployed, operating a day nursery, and finding homes for orphans. The Denver Orphan's Home became a separate organization when it became apparent that the welfare and education of the orphans was too large a task to be undertaken by the society with so many other demands on its resources.

The Ladies Relief Society raised funds and materials through membership fees and donations of money and labor to build a home for orphans. When an offshoot organization, the Denver Orphan's Home Association, was formed in 1881, Eliza was one of ten subscribers who donated $1,000 to launch the effort. After it was decided that half-orphans would be allowed to stay at the home, the number of children cared for grew to twenty-one by the end of 1883. From 1884 through 1897 the number of children in the home fluctuated between fifty and one hundred.

A further manifestation of Eliza Routt's interest in helping young people was evident in her work to expand opportunities for young women. In 1888, Eliza became one of twenty-seven members of the first board of trustees for the newly formed Colorado Woman's College. The stated objective of the board was "to promote, under Christian influence, the education of young women in Literature, Science and Arts."[1] The college educated the women of the state for almost 100 years. In 1982 it became part of the University of Denver.

The apex of Eliza's social and political impact was her involvement in the woman's suffrage movement. After Colorado became a state in 1876, women in favor of suffrage became more vocal. The following year, suffrage for women was voted down by the Colorado legislature by a margin of two to one. Further attempts to pass it failed until 1893. Over the years, Eliza's suffrage work took a great deal of time and energy. John's public support of woman's suffrage on many occasions indicates that he supported her work and her cause wholeheartedly.

At the 1893 annual meeting of the Colorado Woman's Suffrage Association, the name of the organization was changed to the Non-Partisan Suffrage Association of Colorado. An auxiliary organization called the City League of Denver was formed and Eliza Routt was elected president. The emphasis of the state organization

DON'T FORGET THE WOMEN WHEN YOU VOTE ON TUESDAY.
COLORADO
Equal Rights! Equal Responsibilities! Equal Suffrage!

The Colorado press was generally in favor of suffrage for women. This pro-suffrage cartoon ran on the front page of the *Denver Republican*, November 3,1893, three days before the election.

changed from women's rights to equal rights. With direction from the National American Woman Suffrage Association, the Colorado organization became a strong unit of more than one hundred women. In the November 1893 election, the vote was 35,698 to 29,461 in favor of suffrage, making Colorado the second state, after Wyoming, to achieve the progressive distinction of passing women's suffrage into state law.

When the women of Colorado achieved their right to vote, Eliza was chosen to be the first woman to register to vote in the state. Following Eliza's example, women registered, "to exercise this God-given prerogative fearlessly, but with never a selfish motive."[2] As an article in the *Denver Times* stated, "It was eminently fitting that the wife of the first governor of the state, and a lady who has been so intimately connected with all that is best in Denver since the foundation of the state, should be the first woman in Colorado to become [a] fully qualified elector."[3]

Once the vote was won, women sought public office and appointments to decision-making boards. The *Queen Bee* newspaper strongly advocated this involvement. "Women are really needed in office to watch the men, and we will remain barbarians so long as men hold all the offices. The more women we have holding office the better for the country."[4]

In 1895, Eliza led the way again when she became the first woman appointed to the State Board of Agriculture, which established the Colorado State Agricultural College in Fort Collins, Colorado. She began working immediately as chairwoman of a committee to develop a School of Domestic Economy.

On June 5, 1895, Eliza spoke to the board of directors about the importance of establishing the new school of domestic economy. Her report, as published in the board minutes, follows:

> To the Honorable Board of Agriculture of the State of Colorado:
> *(From) Domestic Economy and Library Committee—*
> *Mrs. Routt, A. L. Kellogg, J. S. McClelland—*
>
> The chairman of this committee has corresponded with the Professor of 'Household Economy and Hygiene' in

the Kansas State Agriculture College and gained the information that from very small beginnings in this line of work (begun some twenty years ago) large and satisfactory results are now being obtained.

The twenty years of experience in this department has fully demonstrated its great utility; and now the domestic science department occupies an equal place with the other branches of science in the Kansas Agriculture College.

The different branches of Domestic Economy which are taught in this college are–sewing of all kinds; plain and fancy, with and without the machine; dressmaking; cutting and fitting according to the best systems; and plain and fancy knitting; cooking; by the various methods of making substantial dishes, as well as the forming of dainty dishes; also the making of preserves, jellies, pickles, mince-meat, desserts of all kinds; cakes and plain and fancy breads. The students are taught to wait upon the table, and the art of serving each guest properly.

Dairying is taught by practical work in butter-making; packing and preserving the same; and the influences which affect the quality and quantity of milk. Also the household and factory systems of cheese-making.

All of these branches are taught by practical and experimental work, supplemented by short courses of lectures.

The Chairman of this committee would recommend to this honorable Board the adoption of "Domestic Science" into the course of study of the Colorado Agricultural College, and also that we profit by the experience and example given by our Kansas neighbor, by commencing in a small way and enlarging our facilities as the demand seems to require more tools for work.

In regard to the building to be used by this department, I would suggest the building at the entrance to the College grounds. It would be the most convenient, as it would require but a short time for the students to pass to and from the recitation rooms to this one, and I find a

> very important factor in this work of cooking and serving meals is to have someone for whom to cook and serve; and dinners and lunches must be given and participated in by faculty and students. Often the small sum of 10 cents being charged to cover the cost of material used.
>
> It has occurred to me that, by a liberal use of the white-wash brush and lime that the lower portion of the building might be made clean and relieved from all bad odors; and by the use of cheap paper and paint, the upper portion could be made very home-like and attractive. We would then have an inviting rallying place for much beneficial social life that would have a refining influence that would extend through the whole college life.
>
> *(signed)* Mrs. Eliza F. Routt
> Chairman[5]

The committee's proposal was a tall order, but it was accomplished as presented. Eliza carefully crafted the proposal with the plan to provide affordable meal service for faculty and students to help justify the program's existence. She was thus able to carry through with her vision and convince others to support it.

In addition to creating curriculum and procedures for the new school, Eliza was faced with the task of finding a building for the school and an able educator to head the program. She arranged for space for the school in the horticulture building on campus, and Theodosia G. Ammons was appointed the first instructor of domestic economy at the State Agricultural College. Eliza had worked with Miss Ammons during the suffrage movement, and she knew her to be capable. Her faith was not misplaced.

Eliza's tone with the board grew more forceful and adamant when she approached them about a professorship for the female instructor. At a meeting held on December 12, 1895, Eliza made a strong case for Miss Ammons placement as a part of the regular faculty. After describing the progress of the department, she described the long hours Miss Ammons worked and her earnestness, concluding:

> We are going to ask, and insist, that the Instructor of the Department, Miss Ammons, be made a member of the Faculty. It is necessary that she should be a member of the Faculty and meet with them in order to arrange classes and work in harmony with the other Professors. Surely a Department of such magnitude as the one of Domestic Economy demands the dignity of Professorship. The justice of this request will, we feel assured, be appreciated by every member of the Board.[6]

Eliza's plea was effective. Theodosia Ammons was appointed the first professor of domestic economy at the State Agricultural College. This distinction was followed in 1902 when Eliza obtained the title of Dean of Woman's Work for Theodosia, along with a respectable salary, after more faculty were added to the program. Through their work, the two women gained recognition for the competence of women and expanded educational opportunities for young women of the state.

Eliza Routt and Theodosia Ammons worked together researching the best teaching methods. They used the Department of Household Economy at Kansas State Agricultural College as their model to create an academic domestic training curriculum for their young students. Although quaint and conservative by modern standards, the basic concepts of home economics taught at the school provided a scholastic foundation for the students. Women were thus allowed an important foot in the door of the academic institution and the program grew steadily.

While on the board, Eliza worked to obtain a separate building for the School of Domestic Economy. Her efforts to see that the school had its own building continued even after her resignation from the board. She was able to secure donations from Colorado philanthropist Simon Guggenheim. Five years after her work on the board was complete, the Simon Guggenheim Hall of Household Arts was built and in 1910, the department moved in. Two stained glass windows were installed above the stairway landing, one commemorating Eliza Routt, and the other commemorating Theodosia Ammons.

Denied most respectable jobs in nineteenth-century Denver, women turned to clubs as an outlet for their energy and intellect. Clubs allowed women to unite and work toward positive, productive, and charitable causes. Most women had come to Colorado in the post-Civil War period leaving family and friends behind and arriving with husbands and children in an unfamiliar and unsettled country. They had to endure not only loneliness resulting from the move away from home, but derision from people in eastern cities who saw Colorado as too uncivilized to justify statehood.

Clubs provided like-minded women a place to exchange ideas and work toward solving community problems. Women worked tirelessly to prove the easterners wrong and perhaps to prove to themselves that they were raising families in a civilized community. The camaraderie of such gatherings provided positive benefits to the participants' mental health as well.

Skeptics dismissed Victorian-era women's clubs as ineffective and serving no purpose other than social. The clubs were seen as nothing more than a reason for tea parties and chatter about domestic matters. An April 15, 1894, *Rocky Mountain News* article commented condescendingly on the profusion of clubs: "Denver is a city of women's clubs. There are clubs for the study of every subject with which the feminine mind has ever tried to grapple."

Intelligent women, such as Eliza Routt, found many ways to help improve the community they lived in while their husbands followed political aspirations or dreams of riches. Women's clubs of Denver addressed many issues that improved the newly settled community and molded its character as it grew into a sophisticated capital city. Classical music, artwork, and literary readings were an integral part of meetings and social gatherings. These activities not only boosted their spirits, but also expanded and promoted the arts throughout the community.

An example of this sharing attitude was the Ladies' Loan Exhibition, which was organized in 1879 and believed to be the first of its kind held west of Chicago. Eliza was listed as Mrs. Governor Routt on the ceramic pottery committee. The *Rocky Mountain News*, June 8, 1879, stated:

> The ladies ask and urgently invite the co-operation of each and every citizen of Denver who may possess any rare, curious, unique or antique article of historical interest, or interesting otherwise, to inform any member of the committees, who will make proper arrangements for their safety and exhibition. Special provision has been made for the safety of all articles intrusted [*sic*] to their care. The gentlemen having this matter especially in charge and the proper authorities will be asked to appoint capable and trusty guardians during the continuance of the loan exhibition.

Many organizations benefited from Eliza Routt's involvement. She was a member of the Denver Fortnightly Club, Denver's oldest literary club, for twenty-three years. She also became a charter member of the newly formed Denver Chapter of the Daughters of the American Revolution along with her daughter, Lila.

With her husband, Eliza joined the archery club—an activity considered daring for a woman in Victorian times. Although energetic in her efforts and progressive in her attitude, her style was unremarkable in that she conducted herself without fanfare and without scandal. Under Eliza's management, the lively Routt household, which was in the public eye for so many years, was consistently above reproach, providing no cause for public scrutiny.

Central Christian Church, built in 1901, stood at Sixteenth and Lincoln Streets. John and Eliza were members of the church throughout their years in Denver. *Courtesy Denver Public Library, Western History Department, #00130184.*

Reverend William Bayard Craig, the Routts' minister, friend, and in-law. *Courtesy Cowles Library, Drake University, Des Moines, Iowa.*

ENDNOTES

Chapter 10—Eliza Makes a Difference

1. Wallace B.Turner, *Colorado Woman's College: the Story of a Dream*, (Marceline, Mo.: Walsworth Publishing Co.,1982), 13.
2. *Queen Bee*, #10, (1892) C. N. Churchill, editor. Manuscript collection, Denver Public Library, Western History Department.
3. *Denver Times*, 1 January 1894.
4. *Queen Bee*, #10 (1892).
5. Minutes, State Board of Agriculture, book no. 2: 475-476, Colorado State University Archives.
6. Ibid.

Architect Elijah E. Myers's drawing of the new Colorado State Capitol, 1890.
Courtesy Colorado State Archives.

11

Third-Term Governor

THE 1890S HAVE BEEN REFERRED TO as the Gay Nineties, a period of economic boom in a gaslight setting. Colorado enjoyed this boom, but before the decade was over, the state reeled from the effects of a devastating economic collapse when the price of silver crashed.

At the onset of the decade, the Routts were enjoying the glory and satisfaction of achievements attained through hard work in public office, as well as a settled and comfortable personal life. Life for the Routts revolved around their lively household, business, politics, friends, and family.

John Routt began his third term on the Board of Capitol Managers in 1890, where he had served since 1883. The board's mandate was to supervise and administer the construction of a new state capitol for Colorado, working with a stream of contractors to fulfill the grandiose plans of architect Elijah E. Myers to build a monumental Renaissance-style building. The finest building materials were gathered, with heavy reliance on Colorado resources when available, and first-rate craftsmen were employed. The initial budget for the project was $1 million.

The cornerstone for the new capitol was set on July 4, 1890, amid much celebration. The Masons of Colorado performed a ritual service that included sealing papers and coins into the stone. A profusion of flags, banners, and bunting, a variety of parades, bands, speeches, and fireworks made the Fourth of July celebration especially festive and memorable.

As was his style, John Routt put his heart and soul into his work on the board. He had studied architecture on his own as a young man, and now he could exercise his interest and apply his skills. He supervised expenses, construction, and acquisition of materials scrupulously during the building's construction.

In 1890, as the state's senior statesman, John Routt was recruited once again to run for governor. In the newspaper, he was attacked by his opponents, who called him, "by nature a ruffian, by education a cow-boy."[1] Routt was unruffled by such talk, which to him must have been more a source of amusement than insult.

At the Republican Convention that September, the rhetoric took a much kinder tone, expounding the virtues of their nominee for governor as someone well known, well loved, and trusted by his constituents, with extensive interests in agriculture, mining, and livestock. Routt's supporters were so comfortable with their nominee that in seconding his nomination, he was referred to as "that handsome old rooster, John L. Routt." In reporting the convention, the *Rocky Mountain News*, September 20, 1890, included a cartoon of Routt portrayed as a monkey, using a feather to tickle the nose of his old senate race adversary, Nathaniel Hill, who had retired from politics in 1885.

When it was his turn to speak at the convention, Routt gave the following short speech:

> Mr. Chairman and Gentlemen of the Convention—
> I am at a loss to find words to express my gratitude to this convention for my nomination. I have no speech to make. I am tired, worn out, and I am not a speechmaker anyway. I accept this nomination, knowing full well, if elected, what the people of the state of Colorado expect at my hands. I have the courage, I believe, to do right, so far as I can see the right, making no special promises about anything. I am interested in a good many different enterprises in this state: I propose to protect my taxes, and in doing that I expect to protest yours. [Applause] So far as I can, consistently, or, so far as it becomes my duty to do so, as governor, I expect do everything I can to assist in the development of this house—this, you understand, is on the

hypothesis that I am elected, which, of course, has not yet occurred. [laughter]

Now I thank you, gentlemen, again, but before I quit, I want you to understand, so far as I am concerned, I am at peace with all mankind, and the remainder of the world. I know you want to go home; you do not want to hear me talk; so I will yield, thanking you again. [Loud applause and cheers.][2]

A PARROT AND MONKEY TIME.

Come, birdie come, and live with us,
Drop that reform rot, and don't make a muss;
Boodle's much better than bother and fuss.
Birdie, come off the perch.

Routt won the election to his third two-year term as governor. *Routt Is In,* screamed the inch-high headline on the front page of the *Rocky Mountain News* on the occasion of his third inauguration, January 14, 1891. The inauguration prompted his critics to grumble that John Routt at sixty-five was a relic, an elder statesman beyond his prime who was living in the past. His actions soon proved he was still effective, energetic, and resourceful.

Routt's inauguration was celebrated with parades and speeches, which had become routine in his life, just as Routt's leadership had become routine in Denver and Colorado. As he rode in a carriage drawn by four white horses through downtown Denver, Routt waved and lifted his hat to the crowds. Once inside the Broadway Theater, dignitaries prepared to deliver their speeches while Routt regarded the gathering through his gold-rimmed glasses, twirling his military-style moustache thoughtfully as was his habit. Soon, with raised hand, he solemnly took his oath of office before a hushed crowd that cheered wildly at the conclusion of the ceremony.

Looking on and lending support from their box seats were John Routt's family. Among others in boxes S, T, and U were his daughter, Birdie, and her husband, W. H. Bryant; son John H. Routt; Eliza with their daughter Lila; his daughter, Minnie, with her husband Charles Hartzell; and Eliza's cousin, Emma Craig.

After taking his oath of office, Routt gave a lengthy inaugural address. The speech was mildly criticized in the press for the lack of grace in oratory and lack of volume in his voice, making it difficult for all in attendance to hear. His outlook at the beginning of his third term can be summed up by this excerpt from his speech: "Having heretofore served a term each as territorial and state executive, I feel that the experiences of the past may be of some service to me in the honest endeavor to see that the laws are faithfully executed without fear or favor."[3]

One of the first challenges to face Routt as third-term governor began in 1891. New mineral strikes had caused booms in the Cripple Creek and Creede districts in the southern part of the state. Conflict arose between the townspeople and the newly arrived miners in Creede. During the sudden influx of miners, a squatter's camp appeared and grew on an area designated as state school land. When it was discovered that the state had no clear title from the government, there was a rush by the miners to claim the land.

When in March 1892, an auction sale of the lots was announced, the squatters refused to surrender their illicitly gained property. Led by "Soapy" Smith, a notorious swindler, the unruly group of angry miners, many of them known lawbreakers, threatened violence against the city government. Unable to contain the situation, the sheriff appealed to Governor Routt to send in the National Guard.

Against the advice of his friends, John Routt answered the call by saying, "To h__- with the troops. I'll go myself." Traveling by wagon with officers, guards, and Judge George W. Allen, Governor Routt arrived in Creede during a blinding snowstorm. He stomped into the town hall where Smith's followers were meeting. As he brushed the snow from his coat and wiped his spectacles, Routt stepped up to the platform and said, "H__-, boys. D__- fine day, ain't it?"[4]

The startled but disgruntled men were not impressed and grumbled, "We'll lynch him . . . you old scoundrel."

Ever fearless and censored as usual by the press, Routt said, "What! You will lynch the old man, will you? Well, you are a pretty lot of ____________, ain't you? You are the biggest lot of d__- fools in the United States. I came down here for the purpose of understanding this business, so that when I return to Denver I can get it straightened out. I came down to help you, but if you are going to lynch me you will have murder on your souls and no title to your lot, either."

When the surly group became curious and wanted to hear more, shouting, "Go on, old man," Routt continued, unaffected by the menacing mood that prevailed.

"Maybe you are not such a pack of cussed idiots as I thought you were. The present land board, of which I am a member, is not responsible for the trouble you are having. The sins of political fathers should not be visited upon political children—not a d__-bit of it." Routt assured the men that everything possible would be done to bring justice to the situation. He finished by asking, "Now, do you want to lynch me, or do you want to get a title to your lots?"

When the men responded with, "We'll take the lots," Routt knew he had made his point. The following day, without further incident or bloodshed, the lots were sold to the public at auction for the benefit of the state school fund. The Creede Uprising had been subdued.

By the time the Routts again became the first family of Colorado, they were well accustomed to entertaining important visitors. When President Benjamin Harrison and his wife arrived in Colorado on the Denver and Rio Grande Railroad by special train in May 1891, the Routts were their personal host and hostess, welcoming them with warm hospitality.

With the usual Colorado outpouring of decorations and fanfare, President and Mrs. Harrison were greeted with parades and receptions upon their arrival. A procession paraded through the streets and past the schools of Denver, led by carriages pulled by teams of six high-stepping horses. The first carriage contained President Harrison, Governor Routt, Mayor Rogers, and ex-Senator Hill. Mrs. Harrison and Mrs. Routt occupied the second carriage, along with Senators Teller and Wolcott.

Wives of dignitaries gathered in Eliza Routt's home for a reception in honor of Mrs. Harrison, where Eliza presented her with Rocky Mountain flowers wrapped in satin as a souvenir of her visit. The men gathered separately for lunch at the palatial, newly opened Metropole Hotel. President Harrison sat at a table flanked by state dignitaries that included Governor Routt.

The Routts were part of the entourage as the presidential train traveled through the state. Presidential receptions in Glenwood Springs, Aspen, and Leadville, drew large crowds where a certain amount of lobbying went on. Gifts were presented to the president and his wife, many consisting of commemorative coins and silver decorations, as a way of promoting Colorado's prize mineral.

While stopped at Glenwood Springs, many of the group bathed in the famous hot spring pools. Mrs. Harrison and Mrs. Routt joined the gaiety, feeling either comfortable enough or daring enough to bathe in the public pool, which was closed off from the public for the private gathering. Afterwards, the ladies went sightseeing while the president and the governor rested.

The trip was not without formality and convention. Although they were traveling together, on at least one occasion, when the president wanted to meet with Routt, he sent a telegram.

D. & R. G. Form 5001.—10-90.—1,000,000.

TELEGRAM.

SENT TO	SENDER	RECEIVER	TIME SENT
			M
REC'D FROM	SENDER	RECEIVER	TIME RECEIVED
GS	CK	Q	1745 M.

If service is unsatisfactory, the person to whom addressed should endorse time of delivery and send telegram by mail to Superintendent of Telegraph for investigation.

Time Filed .... M.

Time Delivered .... M.

The time filed must be transmitted as the first words in body of telegram. All railroad messages must be written in ink on these blanks, and those for parties on trains (except trainmen) enclosed in sealed envelope. The exact sending and receiving time, initials of sending and receiving operator, and signal and name of receiving office must be entered in proper spaces in every instance. Operators, after transmitting telegrams which appear unnecessarily long, or that could have been sent by train mail without prejudise to the Company's interests, **are required** to attach original message to Form 4316, and forward to Superintendent of Telegraph.

Clear Creek 5/9 1891

To Gov John L Routt

At C/o F.A. Wadleigh Office.

On 1st No 1 Leadville

The President would like to meet you informally in his Car at about seven fifty and accompany him to breakfast at the Hotel Glenwood at eight Oclock

S.K. Hooper

Telegram from President Harrison to Governor Routt, May 9, 1891, during their excursion into the Colorado mountains. "The President would like to meet you informally in his [railroad] car at about seven fifty and accompany him to breakfast at the Hotel Glenwood at eight o'clock." *Colorado State Archives, file #9353.*

Near the end of Routt's third term, John and Eliza were invited to participate in the Columbian Exposition in Chicago, marking the 400th anniversary of Christopher Columbus's arrival in the New World. Among the splendid delights afforded them in their home state was fabulous entertainment including gondola rides, a giant ferris wheel, and a Wild East and Wild West Show.

As visiting dignitaries, John and Eliza received invitations to official functions and celebrations such as this one to the opening of the Exhibition:

> The honor of the presence of Hon. John L. Routt is requested at a reception to be tendered to the President, Vice-President and ex-Presidents of the United States, the Representatives of Foreign Governments, the

> Governors of the States and Territories, and other distinguished guests at the Auditorium Chicago on Wednesday evening, October 19th, 1892 at 9 o'clock on the occasion of the celebration of the Four Hundredth Anniversary of the discovery of America by Christopher Columbus and the dedication of the World's Columbian Exposition.[5]

Beyond the excitement of the presidential visits and the world's fair, John Routt's third term in office was marred by political controversy and a devastating silver market crash. Two clashing factions in the House of Representatives caused Republican Party infighting. Heated disagreements about committee and Speaker appointments resulted in Supreme Court intervention to decide the validity of the legislature's decisions. The administration was further scrutinized when a Board of Fire and Police Commissioners was created in Denver, transferring power from the mayor's office to the governor's office.

Far worse, however, was the devastating crash in the silver market in 1893, which shook Colorado's economy to its foundation. In spite of western lobbying to dissuade them, Washington legislators chose gold to back the national currency, rather than silver. When the Sherman Silver Mining Act—which insured Colorado silver would be used—was repealed and the government canceled its agreement to buy large amounts of silver from Colorado for currency, the silver market plummeted. The resulting mine closures and unemployment sent the state free falling into economic disaster.

During the resulting depression, men out of work and with time to consider political issues, read the literature provided by suffragists. The prevailing viewpoint was, "Let the Women vote; they can't do any worse than men have."[6] In spite of the negative approach, suffrage was passed into state law. With this grand victory for women, the insults were soon forgotten.

Routt left office as the victory was won. Although his successor, Davis H. Waite, had the honor of signing the women's suffrage proclamation into law, Routt could claim it as a success for his administration since he had worked for so many years to see the law passed. He was outspoken in favor of equal rights for women and supported suffrage while in public office. In light of his continuous backing, women of the state responded with loyalty and admiration for him, notwithstanding his liberal use of profanity. His support was instrumental in the passage of Colorado suffrage, a victory he was able to share with Eliza. She no doubt influenced her husband's unwavering progressive platform.

Routt's successor, Governor Waite, was lukewarm in his support of suffrage but not above capitalizing on the situation. Baker's *History of Colorado* stated, "Waite was mildly in favor of equal suffrage; there is no doubt whatever that he did all he could to capitalize the woman vote in his own behalf, and that immediately after his defeat he denounced woman suffrage as 'a failure' and remained of that opinion."[7] Registering all of those new female voters would be difficult. With Denver's population at about 110,000, Waite ordered a house-to-house canvas by women to register the new voters.

Eliza headed a committee of women drawn from all political parties. They presented a resolution to the state legislature signed by the officers of over 150 suffrage clubs from around the state asking for a constitutional amendment granting nonpartisan voting, using an Australian ballot system with no party affiliation indicated on the ballot. Constituents were alarmed that women would ask for a political change such as a nonpartisan voting system. Nobody could predict how party lines would be affected. Regardless, the new law passed.

As the women became more involved in politics there was a sudden demand for books on civil government and parliamentary law. Eager to exercise their newly won political power, women approached Denver's City Council with an idea to help beautify the city. A new law to build a diagonal tree-lined street "park"—which exists today as Park Avenue—was hastily passed in an attempt to appease the women before they could come up with a more expensive and difficult task.

The council responded with a new law dictating that the newly enfranchised women should show their appreciation for the passage of suffrage by removing their hats in the theater. After the "hat law" passed in Denver without resistance, a wave of similar laws passed across the country, following Colorado's lead.

By 1894, the new state capitol—with its rose onyx, marble, and bronze fixtures—was close to completion at a cost of about $2.8 million. Even though building costs had far surpassed the original million-dollar budget, the committee succeeded in keeping a tight handle on expenditures, and immaculate bookkeeping allowed for proper closure of the project. In addition, the state's economy benefited from the use of local building materials of quarry stone, granite, marble, and onyx, which might have been obtained more cheaply outside of the state. The board also hired the best workers and artisans Colorado had to offer.[8]

Denver City had been the capital of Colorado since 1867 when the state was still a territory. State business was conducted in rented offices at various locations. Before that time, Golden City had been the capital; prior to that, it had been Colorado City, west of Colorado Springs. Colorado state government finally had a home—a solid, proud structure fashioned after the nation's Capitol that would endure as the center of Colorado's government. Although finishing touches were still being completed in 1896, the building was soon functioning as the capital headquarters of the state. The edifice was topped off with a copper dome, which would be replaced in 1908 with 200 ounces of brilliant Colorado gold.

ENDNOTES

Chapter 11—Third-Term Governor

1. Richard D. Lamm, *Pioneers and Politicians*, (Boulder: Pruett Publishing, 1984), 38-40, quoting the *Queen Bee* 17 September 1890.
2. *Rocky Mountain News*, 20 September 1890.
3. *Rocky Mountain News*, 14 January 1891.
4. *Denver Times*, 12 October 1899. See also, Lamm, *Pioneers and Politicians*, 39-40.
5. Colorado State Archives, file #9353.
6. James H. Baker, ed., *History of Colorado*, Vol. 3, (Denver: Linderman Company): 1927, 1121.
7. *Daily News*, "Woman Recognized," 1 January 1894.
8. Colorado State Capitol and the Colorado Board of Capitol Managers, see "Colorado State Capitol Virtual Tour," Colorado State Archives, http://www.state.co.us/gov_dir/gss/archives/cap/gold.htm

The Metropole Hotel opened on Broadway (now Lincoln) near Eighteenth Street in 1892. It was home to the Routts from 1902 until 1907. *Historic Denver News*, February, 1982.

12

A New Century

BY 1896 PUBLIC LIFE for John and Eliza Routt was winding down. They no longer led the state as governor and first lady, but their involvement and interest in state affairs continued even as the world changed around them.

While John finalized loose ends of his formal political career and his work with the Board of Capitol Managers, Eliza embarked on her work on the board of directors of the State Agricultural Board and on a committee to establish the School of Domestic Economy at the State Agricultural College. These were positions she enjoyed, and she frequently rode the train to participate in meetings at the college in Fort Collins, sixty miles north of Denver.

On his seventieth birthday in April 1896, the newspaper quoted Routt as saying, "From now on, I propose to take care of myself so that I may be robust and healthy when I grow old." This sudden interest in health resulted from a scare the previous year when he discovered that travel through higher elevations caused a "sort of a dizziness," chest pains, and shortness of breath from the altitude. He went to Hot Springs, Arkansas, to soak in the hot baths famous for their curative properties. He returned feeling renewed and full of vitality. At his seventieth birthday party, his wife, his children and grandchildren presented him with a huge cake decorated with seventy-one candles—an extra one for "a year to go on."[1]

John retired from the board of capital managers the following year, in 1897. The *Denver Times*, October 12, 1899, commented on his resignation:

> His [Routt's] success as a politician is unparalleled in the history of Colorado, perhaps in the United States. Office holding to him is as much a business as are his extensive mining interests, his stone quarries, and his "cattle upon a thousand hills" …
>
> He retired from office a year ago, when Colorado's "seven-come-eleven" legislature, composed of a heterogeneous mass of Populists, Democrats, Silver Republicans, Administration Republicans and National Silverites repealed the statute providing for a salary of $2,500 a year for each member of the board of capitol managers.
>
> Governor Routt's verbal resignation was emphatic and characteristic. "What in h__- is the state coming to when it expects its officials to work for nothing? I am not a member of a charity organization. If a man's services are worth anything, they are worth paying for."

The Routts continued to live in their home at Fourteenth and Welton Streets. Along with everyone else in the state, the Routts' finances suffered as a result of the Silver Crash of 1893. However, their debts were paid, and their financial interests and investments were diverse enough that they were able to maintain their estate with enough frugality to insure their financial independence and lifestyle.

Not all Colorado residents were as fortunate. Bonanza Kings who had overextended their finances lost entire fortunes during those years, abruptly ending an era of mining dreams in the Centennial State. Ten Denver banks closed their doors in one month.

Routt's contemporary, Horace Tabor, who had over-mortgaged his assets and overstretched his credit in a variety of shaky investments, was wiped out financially. He died of appendicitis on April 3, 1899, leaving his family with little more than memories, a pile of debts, and a played-out silver mine.

The Routts continued to welcome friends during open house hours, which were listed each year in the *Denver Social Year Book.* In 1899, the published register of open houses listed the Gov. and Mrs. J. L. Routt at 1355 Welton St., Friday 3-5, and their daughter, Miss Lila, at 1355 Welton St., Friday 3-5 also.

This listing indicated to friends and guests that they were welcome to drop by unannounced at the times listed, and could expect the Routts to be home to receive them. Visitors left engraved calling cards if the Routts were not at home.

By the late 1890s, "Uncle Johnny" Routt had become a familiar figure, often seen strolling around Denver with the aid of his favorite walking stick, peering over the top of his gold-rimmed spectacles, with little escaping his attention. The *Denver Times*, October 12, 1899, described John Routt at the end of the nineteenth century this way:

> John L. Routt has a square figure with an altitude of 5'2." His head is square as his body and his features are rugged and strong. He has fearless gray eyes. His costume consists of a shirt, black cutaway coat with trousers of the same color, and a black derby hat of the earliest pattern surmounts his square-topped head. Gold-headed canes galore have been presented to him, but these are carefully laid away and he trudges up and down Sixteenth Street with a stout old hickory stick that has been his constant companion for a quarter of a century. As he clings to this old stick, so does he cling to his old friends and to the memory of those who were his friends before they died.
>
> His English is direct and emphatic, but the chief characteristic is an utter disregard for the Third Commandment. Profanity with him is a language that has been reduced to a science.

The 1900 Denver census listed the Routt household as follows: John L. Routt (74), Eliza F. Routt (61), Lila E. Routt (19), John H. Routt (36), Annie A. Routt (32), Mary Breedlove (46, a servant from Virginia). Routt's son John and his wife, Annie, were back in residence with the elder Routts and were no longer living on their ranch near Fort Collins. John's occupation was listed as a granite dealer.

Francis T. Bruce and his wife, Ellen, were not listed as part of the Routt household. Bruce had been hired as a custodian at the new capitol, where he worked until his death in 1917. He had been with the Routts in Colorado since their arrival from Washington, D.C., in 1875, and he remained a close personal friend. Bruce had been with the family during John's first marriage, and he had been present while all of the Routt children were growing up.

In ensuing years, Bruce continued to be a loyal friend to John, who enjoyed his company and frequently encouraged Bruce to visit with him. When the elderly ex-governor went walking, he enjoyed strolling to the new capitol, which he had so carefully overseen to completion. When Bruce saw Routt approaching, he would immediately leave his duties as custodian to welcome Routt, escort him around the building, and walk with him until he was safely home again. Bruce's time away from his duties was condoned and encouraged by administrators of the capitol out of respect and courtesy to the ex-governor.

As Colorado raced ahead into the twentieth century, Eliza and John were slowing down. They had helped Colorado become a prospering state and could look back with pride at their many accomplishments. John had spent most of the past half century in public office. Eliza had served in many civic positions over the same time period.

On the recommendation of his doctor, John made plans to travel in Europe hoping that a more humid climate would relieve his sciatica, a condition that causes sharp pain in the hip. On May 22, 1900, John, Eliza, and nineteen-year-old Lila sailed to Europe, where they planned to reside for a few years.

The Routts traveled around Europe, with Paris as their home base. In Paris, they enjoyed attractions such as the Eiffel Tower, completed in 1889. Lila stayed busy studying vocal music with a teacher named Mademoiselle Richard. Her musical training inspired her lifelong interest in performing as a singer and supporting music in Denver.

Two years after leaving Colorado, Routt wrote his friend General John C. Kennedy expressing his desire to return. The text of the letter was reprinted in the *Denver Times*, April 22, 1902.

We (meaning Mrs. Routt, his daughter Lila and himself) expect to sail from Liverpool, England, May 21 (1902) next on the 'Celtic' on our return to the United States and our beloved home state of Colorado. Please tell the old friends that you have heard from me, that I am in good health for one of my age, and that I hope to be home about the 1st of June this year.

I love to hear from my old friends and from our home. I am somewhat lonesome here, as I cannot speak French. I run in a crowd by myself, not many to talk to or to sing with, so I might say I am homesick, and have been so ever since I came here, not that Paris is not a very interesting city, for it is, but the people are so different from our Americans.

As you know, I am very fond of our beloved state, our baby state, the one that we have done so much to help it, develop its resources, build its cities and towns and its churches and school houses, as well as every other needed improvement. I say, God bless Colorado and her people. I see our people are wild over oil and sugar beets. I do hope that the oil business will pay big; as to the sugar beet, that it will be very profitable in the near future. When the resources of Colorado are fully developed she will be the greatest state in the union.

Extended travels and the change of climate had energized John and Eliza, and they came back feeling stronger. Doctors had counseled John to stay in a damp climate, and there had been plenty of that in rainy Paris. Despite the advice, the lure of Colorado was too great and they returned home.

Denver had changed with the advent of the new century. During their two-year absence, formerly elegant Governor's Row on Fourteenth Avenue had been transformed. Low, flat commercial buildings used as physician's offices surrounded the old Routt mansion.

While they were in Europe, their house had been leased and was unavailable. The Metropole Hotel, built in 1891, provided a convenient and comfortable residence. Located near the corner of

Broadway and Eighteenth Streets, the towering nine-story hotel faced the Brown Palace Hotel across the street. The building also housed the Broadway Theater.

The décor and amenities in the Metropole were similar to those of its neighbor across the street, and advertising for both edifices boasted of being "absolutely fire proof." Those words were painted in huge letters on the south side of the Metropole. When it opened, the Metropole was operated on the European Plan, which did not include meals in its rental rate, although the hotel had an elegant restaurant and café offering fine dining, with place settings of beautiful china and linen. Ads proclaimed the hotel was "famed for excellence of its Cuisine and Service, and combining all the comforts of home, your surroundings dispelling any feeling of being in a public hotel."[2]

H. C. Brown's Palace Hotel, now known as the Brown Palace, opened in 1892 and operated on the American Plan, with meals included. The Brown Palace was managed by Horace Tabor's son N. Maxcy Tabor, and his partner, William H. Bush, who also managed the Metropole with Otto Kappler. Daily rates per room for the Metropole in 1892 were: twenty rooms at $1.50, thirty rooms at $2.00, twenty rooms at $2.50, twenty rooms at $3.00, sixty rooms at $3.50, and upward. Across the street, rates at the Brown Palace were almost double but that rate included meals.

The *Denver Times*, April 28, 1891, eloquently described the Metropole Hotel when it opened:

> The building is nine stories high, constructed of pressed brick and trimmed with ornamental terra-cotta with steel girders. The partitions, floors, ceilings and walls are of hollow tile, and the stairways and elevators are iron and bronze, making it an absolutely fire-proof building.
>
> In regard to the sanitary, heating and lighting arrangements no money has been spared to secure perfection. The entire building will be heated by steam, a radiator being placed in each apartment; also an open grate for those who prefer it. The lighting will be by electricity, the fixtures being electric and gas combined.

> The woodwork will be in antique oak, natural mahogany, cherry and oak. Walls and ceilings are of adamant plaster. The lower floors, containing offices, restaurant, café, etc., will be finished in handsome marbles and tilings. The furniture, of the latest improved design and finish, will correspond with the woodwork of the floor upon which it is placed, as will also the Asminster carpets on every floor.
>
> The dining rooms will be marvels of elegance, luxury, and comfort. The finest linens, chinaware, glassware and silverware will be used. Otto Keppler, who has for many years been connected with the Windsor will have general supervision of the cuisine. All the employees around the place will be uniformed. The hotel will be run on the European plan and it is the aim of the management to make the 'Metropole' one of the most perfect hostelries in the United States. Charles Elmendorf, an old attaché from the Windsor, will be head clerk.

In choosing the Metropole for their residence, the Routts were surrounded by reminders of glorious times during the past decade, such as President Harrison's visit. They used the income from their leased mansion to cover their expenses, and the hotel provided the aging Routts with a comfortable residence close to church, friends, the theater, and the capitol. Eliza was suffering from the onset of diabetes, and the roomy mansion at Fourteenth and Welton would have been too much for her to manage. The hotel residence provided a comfortable and cozy alternative. Although the family continued to own the mansion, John and Eliza never again resided there.

Lila made her social debut shortly after the family's return to Denver. She was presented to Denver society at a fittingly festive affair in the home of Birdie May Bryant, Lila's half-sister from John Routt's first marriage.

Although she was not well, Eliza Routt was still interested in socializing and had taken advantage of her time in Paris to acquire a fine new gown. She dressed up to celebrate her daughter's special party. As was their habit, the press went into great detail in describing her dress as "an exquisite Paris creation of lavender crepe de chine, trimmed with Irish point lace, and diamond ornaments." Lila was the center attraction in "white Swiss, and (she) has a dozen bouquets to choose from—sent by admirers." The newspaper described Lila as charming, well-bred, and unaffected.[3]

Among those helping Eliza, Lila, and Birdie with the party was Eliza's cousin Emma Craig. Her husband, the Reverend William Bayard Craig, had taken a position as chancellor at Drake University in Des Moines, Iowa, in 1897. After serving there for five years, they had recently returned to Colorado and lived in Pueblo.

The Metropole Hotel was a short walk from the Central Christian Church on South Broadway which continued to be an important part of the Routts' lives. An elaborate celebration was held for the church's twelfth anniversary in December 1902. The church had come a long way since Reverend Craig held services for its early congregations in a tent at the south end of town. Craig continued to be friends with the Routts and returned to celebrate the growth of the church with them.

Lila continued to be the center of the Routt household, staying close to her parents throughout her young adulthood. Eliza and Lila became charter members of the Denver chapter of the Daughters of the American Revolution, founded on March 10, 1904. Their Revolutionary War ancestor was Eliza's great-great grandfather on her mother's side, Archibald Edmonson (or Edmondson), a colonial patriot who enlisted from Maryland.[4]

As for John Routt's alliances, he was a member of the McLean County (Illinois) Post No. 16 of the Grand Army of the Republic (G. A. R.) as a result of his Civil War service. He was also a member of Masonic Union Lodge No. 7 in Denver and a charter member of the Denver Club.

By 1905, Eliza's participation on the State Board of Agriculture, which required the tiring train rides to meetings in Fort Collins, became too strenuous for her. The April 25, 1905, minutes of the State Board of Agriculture recorded her resignation.

Gentlemen,—

I regret exceedingly that on account of continued illness in my family, causing my inability to attend the meetings has forced the conclusion upon me that I must sever my connection with your Honorable Board.

The attendance at the Board meetings for so many years, has given me very great pleasure, and (I) will always cherish the memory of the cordial greetings and kindly consideration accorded me by every member of the Board. So great is my interest in the Domestic Science Department that I must ask the united and friendly interest and consideration of every member of your Honorable Board in this Department.

Again with feeling akin to lonesomeness, I send in my resignation.

Very respectfully,
Eliza F. Routt

Eliza's resignation was accepted, and a resolution to convey regrets was drawn up. Her vague reference to family health reflected her own problems as well as John's. When John and Lila traveled to Puerto Rico that year to visit Minnie's husband, Charles V. Hartzell, Eliza stayed home.

After returning from Paris and re-entering the lively social scene, Lila, 25, was courted by Dr. Edward Welles Collins, a popular young throat specialist. They soon made plans to marry, and her parents were able to share her anticipation as she planned her wedding. Lila and Edward kept arrangements simple, yet elaborate enough to accommodate hundreds of guests from throughout the state.

On Lila's wedding day, the Reverend Craig officiated. He performed an Episcopal service at the evening ceremony on February 8, 1906, at the Central Christian Church, which was decorated with an abundance of flowers and palms. The bride carried pink roses and had a wreath of pink rosebuds in her hair, her veil held in place by a sunburst of diamonds. Her satin gown was decorated with family heirloom lace. Lila's niece—her half-sister Birdie's little daughter, Lila Bryant—was the flower girl and also carried the ring.

Even though Lila's wedding celebration was subdued and simple due to her parents' poor health, it was declared "one of the more beautiful and interesting weddings which have taken place in the city."[5] Her husband's brother walked her down the aisle, as hundreds of their Colorado friends looked on. Lila's cousin Metella Ives of St. Louis was her only attendant, and there was no reception after the wedding.

Lila and her new husband left that evening for a trip to Chicago, Cincinnati, and other eastern cities. When they returned to Denver to begin their new life together, they moved into their own home at the Maples Apartments, located at 1755 Grant Street, two blocks from her parents' residence at the Metropole Hotel.

The Routt family experienced a tragic loss when later in the spring, Lila's flower girl, Lila Bryant, died. The little four-year-old succumbed to acute tuberculosis and meningitis on May 13, 1906. The inscription on her gravestone in the Routt plot at Riverside Cemetery reads, "Lila Routt Bryant, 1901-1906, 'Jesus wants me for a sunbeam'."

The world was changing fast. When the Routts moved into the Metropole Hotel, horses still pulled carriages up and down Broadway and Lincoln past the Metropole and Brown Palace hotels. The changeover from horses to horseless carriages was beginning, and the complete transition to the newly popular automobile was underway. Before the decade was past, the sights and sounds from the Metropole's windows would change forever.

ENDNOTES

Chapter 12—A New Century

1. *Denver Republican*, 26 April 1896, 5.
2. *Denver Hotel Bulletin*, 16 September 1892 and 17 April 1893. Brown Palace Archives.
3. *Denver Times*, 28 October 1902.
4. Colorado State Society of D.A.R., *Colorado D.A.R. Member and Ancestor List*, (Bountiful, UT: Family History Publishers, 1981), 115. Eliza's D.A.R. membership number was #46572; Lila's was #46573.
5. *Denver Times*, 8 February and 9 February 1906.

Eliza Routt Memorial Window, Guggenheim Hall, Colorado State University, installed 1910, commemorates Eliza's work in establishing the School of Domestic Economy. *Photographer: Joyce Lohse (2000).*

13

End of an Era

On March 22, 1907, barely a year after Lila's wedding, at seven o'clock on a Friday morning, Eliza Pickrell Routt's life came to an end. Lila and Edward had moved into the Sherman Apartments at 1720 Sherman Street, a block from the Metropole Hotel. It was at Lila's apartment, surrounded by family, that Eliza died, at age sixty-eight from liver disease and complications from diabetes.

A large memorial service was attended by a gathering of citizens whose lives she had touched. Her close friend and cousin Emma Craig had died a few months earlier, and it was Emma's husband, Reverend Craig, who gave Eliza's eulogy at the Central Christian Church. It was difficult for him to speak about the two women who were constant companions in daily life, more like sisters than cousins. He was so overcome with emotion that he broke down during the eulogy, moving many in the congregation to tears.

During the funeral service, Reverend Craig said of Eliza:

> Memory will hold Mrs. Routt in continued companionship at her best and noblest self, as she was in all her queenly powers as the governor's wife, the charming hostess of great state and social functions; a leader in philanthropic enterprises; an active member on educational boards and of literary and charitable organizations, and always as the queenly, gracious, cultured and best exponent of all that was noblest and best in our modern civic life …

She was eminent and commanding in all her traits of character. She was a fine executive and her power as a leader was due not less to her reasonableness, her fine sense of justice and her ability to win the love and esteem of her associates, than to her fixity of purpose and commanding personality.

The fine qualities in her character were manifest in her selection of friends. She found them among the high and the lowly, the rich and the poor, stately, and loyal to the proprieties and conventionalities of her own social position, without the slightest show or feeling or condescension, she recognized worth and integrity wherever she found it in every walk of life …

Three times Governor Routt was chief executive of Colorado and during three terms of office and between times Mrs. Routt fulfilled the duties of 'first lady' with remarkable ability and generous hospitality.[1]

After Eliza's death, Lila sent the following note to the Secretary of the State Board of Agriculture:

My dear Mr. Hawley:

Will you please express my sincere thanks to the Board and Faculty of the College for the very beautiful wreath that they so kindly sent to my mother.

She was keenly interested in every thing about the College and their remembrance of her has greatly pleased and touched me.

Very sincerely,
Lila Routt-Collins[2]

The board responded to the loss by entering a proclamation into its records. The proclamation, dated April 20, 1907, read:

Resolved that in her [Mrs. Routt's] death the state has sustained the loss of a noble woman whose entire life during her long years of residence in Colorado was devoted to conserving and extending the best of social influences; whose relations to life as a wife, a mother and a member of various Christian and social and civic organizations, command unbounded confidence and admiration; and whose work in connection with this institution, especially in the creation and maintenance of its Domestic Science Department, and for all other factors that were for the benefit of the young women and young men of Colorado, is gratefully recognized and remembered by this Board.[3]

On the occasion of Eliza's death, the *Denver Times*, March 22, 1907, used its front page to express the respect and affection the citizens of Colorado held for their First Lady.

Death of Mrs. Routt

One of the spirits which gave warmth and light and homelike grace to Colorado during its passage from the old pioneer days into the new full-blown era was Mrs. Eliza Routt, whose death at far too early an age has saddened the hearts of a multitude today.

Her husband was the last territorial governor and the first to serve under the state government. At the beginning of the first of three terms Governor Routt brought her to the state a bride.

The first lady of the state soon won that place in fact as well as in name. Gracious, gentle, hospitable, knowing no lines or clique or class, she soon made all the state feel that in the home of the state's executive dwelt one who would represent all that was best and noblest in the state.

Unpretentious and unassuming, this wife of the governor was yet able by the strength of her personal charm and influence to give vital impetus to every progressive and helpful movement of the new city and state.

The Old Ladies' home, the Orphans' home, the woman's suffrage movement—all of these and many other efforts received from her invaluable assistance.

But more than any specific task was the pervading inspiration of a great-hearted woman—a woman loyal, faithful and strong as wife, mother, friend and the kindly, helpful neighbor to all her world—and that world was large.

While the people of Colorado said good-bye to their original first lady, the news of her passing was kept from her husband. With his own health deteriorating rapidly, his family and physicians were afraid that the news of Eliza's death would be more than he could bear. He was simply told, "She has gone away for a short time, and will be with you soon again."[4]

Those carefully chosen words proved true in a sense. After Eliza died, John Routt lost interest in life and sat waiting quietly for his to end. At age 81, he was ready. He would not even enter into conversation when his old friend, Francis Bruce, came to visit.

The wait for death was over at 12:30 a.m. on August 13, 1907. Lila and Edward cared for John at their residence, and it was there that he died, as Eliza had five months earlier. His children surrounded him at Lila's home. Bruce was present, waiting close by to lend comfort and assistance to the family. He wept openly over the passing of his longtime friend.

John Routt's funeral was a grand tribute. Flags flew at half mast and government offices closed early. A horse-drawn hearse delivered his casket to the capitol. Pallbearers carried the casket into the west hallway where it remained for two hours while the public

SORROWING FRIENDS ATTEND THE FUNERAL CEREMONIES OVER THE BODY OF LATE GOVERNOR ROUTT AT THE STATE CAPITOL

Pallbearers taking the casket of governor Routt from the hearse to the Capitol building, where it lay in state. Photograph and caption from the *Denver Times, August 16, 1907*.

walked past paying their respects. The funeral was held at the Central Christian Church where Eliza and John had membership for so many years. The *Denver Times*, August 16, 1907, reported, "A simple and touching service was conducted by the Masonic lodge of Denver." The graveside service at Riverside Cemetery north of Denver was attended by the immediate family.

The Routts' obituaries state that they were buried in Fairmount Cemetery, which has led to some confusion. That burial location was also entered onto their death certificates. A review of the interment records of Fairmount and Riverside cemeteries solves the mystery. Fairmount Cemetery Company bought Riverside Cemetery in 1900, thus becoming Riverside's parent company. When Eliza died, her remains were placed in a vault at Fairmount Cemetery, then were removed and buried next to her husband's grave at Riverside Cemetery on August 31, 1907, two weeks after his funeral. Arrangements, payments, and improvements to Lot 114 in Block 6 at Riverside likely were not finalized by the family until both Routts were deceased.

The Routt estate was little more than the amount John turned over to Eliza upon striking it rich in Leadville. Just as other Bonanza Kings had taken a hard hit during the Silver Crash of 1893, so had the Routts. The *Denver Times*, August 13, 1907, stated, "Although once a millionaire, the estate of Routt has depreciated greatly during the last years of his life, and it is now reported to valued at little in excess of $100,000. After the death of her mother, Lila Routt-Collins, begotten of the second marriage, was named to share the property of her mother, in whose name much of her father's property had been placed equally with her father."

The Routt mansion was the main asset remaining from their fortune. Lots around the grounds of the property had been previously sold off as sites for medical offices. A note written to Eliza Routt at the Metropole Hotel from her lawyer, Charles A. Stokes, listed three properties requiring 1904 taxes to be paid, including the aging mansion. This would indicate that Eliza had held on to and continued to manage at least a portion of their real estate holdings. The lots were at 2541 Welton, 2130 High, and the mansion property at Fourteenth and Welton, for which over $1,000 in taxes were owed. Little else was left in the way of an inheritance.

On May 3, 1907, a probate court hearing determined that John was no longer mentally competent to handle his financial affairs. Their property and deeds had previously been turned over to Lila. Another daughter, Emma Butler, was named as conservatrix of the estate. Following Eliza's death, revenue from the Routts' rental properties was paid to Lila to be used for the care of Governor Routt. Upon his death, the property belonged to her.

Sketch of John Routt in retirement that accompanied his obituary in the *Denver Times*, August 13, 1907.

Endnotes

Chapter 13—End of an Era

1. *The Daily News*, 25 March 1907, 1-2. (*Denver Times*, *Denver Post*, and the *Denver Republican* also published obituaries.)
2. Minutes. State Board of Agriculture (11 April 1907): 98. Colorado State University Archives.
3. State Board of Agriculture to Lila Routt-Collins, 20 April 1907. MSS 977, Stephen H. Hart Library, Colorado Historical Society.
4. *Daily News*, 25 March 1907.

Routt Hall, Colorado State University, was renamed in 1999 to honor Eliza Routt for her years of service on the State Board of Agriculture. *Photographer: Joyce Lohse (2000).*

14

The Routt Legacy

JOHN AND ELIZA ROUTT left a legacy of memories and rich history in the state they loved, a solid, new state capitol, their family and descendants, and new freedom and opportunity won for women. Lila's family was just beginning, with the adoption of a daughter, Dorothia, in 1910, and the birth of a second daughter, Lila, in 1918. Daughter Lila would have many productive years in Denver. She was known for her perfect soprano voice and sang publicly in Denver at places such as the original Elitch Gardens. She was also one of three founders of the Denver Civic Symphony.

Although Lila Routt's marriage to Edward did not endure, the family continued through her children, and through the families of the children from John Routt's first marriage to Hester Ann Woodson.[1] Lila died of a heart attack on June 30, 1947. She is buried in the family plot at Riverside Cemetery in Denver.

Of the children from John Routt's first marriage, Julie "Minnie" Routt was married to Charles V. Hartzell and died during childbirth in 1891. Hartzell then married Ida Jones, Eliza Routt's cousin from Decatur, Illinois, in 1894. President Theodore Roosevelt appointed Hartzell secretary of state to Puerto Rico in 1901.

Frank C. Routt continued to raise cattle at the ranch in northern Colorado and worked in mining in Denver and Cripple Creek. He fought illness his whole life and died of Bright's disease with deteriorating mental health in Pueblo, Colorado, in 1912. He was survived by two sons from his marriage to Kate.

Photograph of Lila Routt-Collins at age 45 was published in the *Denver Post*, Society Page, August 1, 1926.

John H. Routt was married to Annie A. Wright and worked in livestock and a stone quarry business in Denver. He died in 1913 in Goldfield, Nevada.

Birdie May Routt married William H. Bryant, a Denver city attorney and law partner of former Governor Charles S. Thomas. She survived her husband by only one year, succumbing to appendicitis in 1915, and was survived by three children. One of Birdie's children was Minnie Lou Bryant. Her life with her second husband, Frank Wilbur "Spig" Wead, was the subject of a 1957 feature film entitled *The Wings of Eagles*, starring John Wayne. Actress Maureen O'Hara portrayed Minnie. The Weads' infant son is buried in the Routt family plot in Riverside Cemetery in Denver.

Emma Routt was married to Frederick A. Butler, who worked on the board of public works in Denver. She died in 1922.

Few landmarks and artifacts from the Routts' early days remain. Their mansion was sold in 1909 and torn down shortly thereafter. The residential district of the Routt mansion and the splendid homes on what was called Governor's Row along Fourteenth Avenue and Welton Street is now the location of the Colorado Convention Center and the Denver Athletic Club, in the heart of downtown Denver.

Walter Scott Cheesman, who died before its completion, built the current Governor's Mansion, located at 400 East Eighth Avenue, in 1908. His family sold it to businessman Claude K. Boettcher, who decorated it with art objects collected from around the world. It became the executive residence in 1959. Tours of the mansion give a sense of the décor, lifestyle, and history of Colorado's governors in its furnishings.

A room in the Governor's Mansion has a display of photos of Colorado's first ladies on one wall and Colorado's governors on a facing wall. John and Eliza Routts' photos are included in the display. A challenging two-year hunt in 1968 turned up the photos of all of Colorado's first ladies to complete the unique display.

A preserved house in downtown Denver provides a wonderful example of a home built while Routt was mayor of Denver. The Byers-Evans House, at the corner of Thirteenth Avenue and Bannock Street, has been restored by the Colorado Historical Society and is open for tours. The house was built in 1883 by William Byers, who was the first publisher of the *Rocky Mountain News*. In 1889, Byers sold the house to the William Gray Evans family. Eliza Routt served on boards and committees, and socialized with Elizabeth Byers and Margaret Gray Evans. Perhaps Eliza and John visited the house during their lifetimes.

The Byers-Evans House is unique in that its fixtures and furnishings are original and reminiscent of the era in which it was built. One feature of particular interest is the fireplace in the parlor. It contains a border of tiles depicting scenes from *Aesop's Fables*, which were popular at the time, and are similar to those shown in the Thomas Nast drawing of Lila in front of the Routt's hearth in *Harper's Weekly*.

Another Victorian home open to the public in Denver is the Molly Brown House at 1340 Pennsylvania Street. Margaret Tobin Brown was the wife of another Leadville Silver King, James J. Brown. They came to Denver to live and enjoy their wealth. Mrs. Brown became famous for her spunk and activism, and later for her heroic efforts as a survivor of the *Titanic* when it sank in 1912. Her house is an interesting and opulent example of Victorian décor. Mrs. Brown and Mrs. Routt could have crossed paths; they were both active in the women's suffrage movement, but there is no record that they were acquainted. The Browns were no relation to Henry C. Brown, who built the Brown Palace Hotel.

The Brown Palace is probably the most famous Denver landmark left from the late nineteenth century. Built in 1892, the famous hotel is the destination of people from all over the world and features elegant Victorian décor and gracious service. The Brown's neighbor across the street, the Metropole Hotel, John and Eliza Routts' final home, no longer exists.

Buildings that housed the original state offices used by Governor Routt in Denver's lower downtown district are gone. However, the solid state capitol, for which John Routt lovingly and diligently supervised construction, stands proudly overlooking Denver and vibrates with government activity and tourist visits. The building's interior of marble and brass are constantly shined and maintained in

A stained glass portrait of John Routt was installed in the Colorado State Capitol Senate Chambers in 1909. *Photographer: Joyce Lohse (1999)*.

brilliant condition. A stained glass window portraying John Routt seated in his study is part of Colorado's Hall of Fame, located on the back wall of the Senate chambers. The window was installed in September 1909, two years after Routt's death. Manufactured by the Copeland Art Glass Manufacturing Company, the window took four months to complete at a cost of $1,000.

In addition to the stained glass window portrait of Routt, his name is chiseled on the granite cornerstone on the northeast corner of the capitol. The wording carved into the cornerstone's east side reads, "Laid by the N W Grand Lodge A F & A M of Colorado, July 4, 1890, A L 5490." Carved into the north side of the stone are these words: "Erected by acts of the fourth and seventh general assemblies of the State of Colorado, approved Feb. 11, 1883 & April 1, 1893. Board of Capitol Managers, Job A. Cooper, Governor, John L. Routt, Chas. J. Hughes, Jr., Otto Mears, Benj. F. Crowell. E. E. Myers, arch., H. Lueders, sey., Peter Cumry, sup'l."

While in public office, Routt used a remarkable hand-carved walnut desk, described as six feet in height, with locking mail slots built into the front cabinetry. From all indications, the description and appearance of the desk matches that of a Wooten-style desk. President Ulysses S. Grant owned one, and it is plausible that John Routt fancied the walnut beauty, chock full of slots and pigeonholes, and decided to procure one of his own. At one time, Routt's desk was owned by the Colorado Historical Society, but the whereabouts and the fate of the desk is now unknown.

In Fort Collins, Eliza Routt is memorialized by a stained glass window in Guggenheim Hall at the State Agricultural College, now known as Colorado State University. The window is located on the landing wall between the first and second floor of that building and bears a wreath and the inscription, "In memory of Eliza F. Routt." Next to it is a similar window, "In Memory of Theodosia G. Ammons," first instructor for the School of Domestic Economy, who also died in 1907.

Leadville celebrates its mining heritage by preservation of its mining district and historic buildings. Tours of preserved buildings, museums, and the mining district are available to visitors. Although the mines on Carbonate Hill are gone or in ruins, H. A. W. Tabor's Matchless Mine has been restored and is open to the public for guided tours. The cabin adjacent to the mine, where Baby Doe Tabor spent her final years, is a small museum. The hoist housing is part of the museum, and displays restored apparatuses and other mining equipment.

Colorado recognized the many contributions of John Routt by naming Routt County in northwestern Colorado after him. Routt National Forest near Steamboat Springs in Routt County is also named in his honor.

In the fall of 1999, Eliza Routt was again memorialized when a building at Colorado State University was dedicated in her honor. Routt Hall at the corner of College and Laurel Streets in Fort Collins now bears the Routt name in honor of Eliza's contributions to the State Board of Agriculture during Colorado State University's early years. A photographic portrait of Eliza is displayed in the hallway of the building.

The enduring legacy of John and Eliza Routt is their commitment to Colorado and their many contributions during those fragile early years of Colorado's history. Their love for their adopted state is made visible by their work and dedication to the birth of the state. An important part of a glorious past, the Routts helped create a foundation from which Colorado would grow and thrive.

The Metropole Hotel was located south of Trinity Methodist Church on Broadway (later Lincoln). The church still stands, as does the Brown Palace Hotel shown opposite the Metropole in the photograph. *Courtesy Denver Public Library, Western History Department*, MCC-*1175*. Photographer: L.C. McClure, ca. 1900.

ENDNOTES

Chapter 14—The Routt Legacy

1. Information about the Routts' descendants drawn from: *Denver Times*, 14 June 1915 (Birdie Routt Bryant obituary); *Rocky Mountain News* and *Denver Post* 4 May 1912 (Frank C. Routt obituary); *Denver Times*, 26 March 1907; Merry Lynn Lisle, *John Long Routt Relationship List*, 1990; *Portrait and Biographical Record of Denver and Vicinity Colorado*, 1989; William N. Byers, *Encyclopedia of Biography of Colorado*, 1901; Gravestones, Riverside Cemetery, Denver, Colorado; Correspondence and conversation with Dorothy O'Connell, (February 1999), and with Lila Nobles, (March 2000).

Colorado Governors

	COLORADO TERRITORY	
1861-1862	Gilpin, William	R
1862-1865	Evans, John	R
1865-1867	Cummings, Alexander	R
1867-1869	Hunt, Alexander C.	R
1869-1873	McCook, Edward	R
1873-1874	Elbert, Samuel H.	R
1874-1875	McCook, Edward	R
1875-1876	**Routt, John L.**	**R**
	STATE OF COLORADO	
1877-1879	**Routt, John L.**	**R**
1879-1883	Pitkin, Frederick W.	R
1883-1885	Grant, James B.	D
1885-1887	Eaton, Benjamin H.	R
1887-1889	Adams, Alva	D
1889-1891	Cooper, Job A.	R
1891-1893	**Routt, John L.**	**R**
1893-1895	Waite, Davis H.	P
1895-1897	McIntyre, Albert W.	R
1897-1899	Adams, Alva	D
1899-1901	Thomas, Charles S.	D
1901-1903	Orman, James B.	D
1903-1905	Peabody, James H.	R

1905	Adams, Alva	D
1905	Peabody, James H.	R
1905-1907	Jesse F. McDonald	R
1907-1909	Henry A. Buchtel	R
1909-1913	Shafroth, John F.	D
1913-1915	Ammons, Elias M.	D
1915-1917	Carlson, George A.	R
1917-1919	Gunter, Julius C.	D
1919-1923	Shoup, Oliver H.	R
1923-1925	Sweet, William H.	D
1925-1927	Morley, Clarence J.	R
1927-1933	Adams, William H.	D
1933-1937	Johnson, Edwin C.	D
1937	Talbot, Ray H.	D
1937-1939	Ammons, Teller	D
1939-1943	Carr, Ralph L.	R
1943-1947	Vivian, John C.	R
1947-1950	Knous, William L.	D
1950-1951	Johnson, Walter W.	D
1951-1955	Thornton, Daniel I. J.	R
1955-1957	Johnson, Edwin C.	D
1957-1963	McNichols, Stephen L. R.	D
1963-1973	Love, John A.	R
1973-1975	Vanderhoof, John D.	R
1975-1987	Lamm, Richard D.	D
1987-1999	Romer, Roy R.	D
1999-	Owens, Bill	R

D = *Democrat*, P = *Populist*, R = *Republican*

Timeline

1825–William Elkin, Eliza Pickrell's grandfather, settles in Sangamon County, Illinois.

1826–John Long Routt is born in Eddyville, Kentucky.

1831–The Pickrell brothers settle in Sangamon County, Illinois.

1834–Benjamin Franklin Pickrell marries Mary Ann Elkin.

1835–John Routt's family settles in Illinois.

1838–Benjamin Franklin Pickrell, Eliza's father, dies.

1839–Eliza Franklin Pickrell is born five months after her father's death.

1840–Eliza's mother, Mary Ann, marries Abner Riddle.

1842–Mary Ann Riddle dies three months after giving birth to a son. Eliza is sent to live with her Elkin grandparents near Springfield, Illinois.

1845–John Long Routt marries Hester Ann Woodson in Bloomington, Illinois. He works as a carpenter and they start a family.

1850–McLean County, Illinois census lists John Routt (age 24), his wife, Hester Ann, and son, Francis (3). Sangamon County census lists Eliza (11) in William Elkin's household.

1854–John Routt holds his first public office as alderman in Bloomington, Illinois.

1860–Sangamon County census lists William Elkin, Elizabeth, William A., and Eliza F. (21). John Routt is elected sheriff of McLean County.

1862–John Routt enlists in the Union Army. He wins the favor of General Grant through his resourcefulness and bravery.

1865–John Routt is honorably discharged from the Union Army. He is elected county treasurer in Bloomington, Illinois, for two terms.

1867–The Elkin family moves to Decatur, Illinois. Denver becomes the capital city of Colorado Territory.

1869–General Ulysses S. Grant is elected president of the United States and serves through 1877.

1870–John Routt is appointed marshal in the Southern Illinois District.

1871–John Routt is appointed second assistant postmaster general and moves with his family to Washington, D.C. His mother Martha Haggard dies.

1872–John Routt's wife Hester Ann, dies leaving him with five children. Elizabeth Elkin, Eliza's grandmother dies.

1874–After a whirlwind courtship, Eliza Pickrell marries John Routt in Decatur, Illinois.

1875–John Routt is appointed territorial governor of Colorado and moves to Denver City with his family.

1876–Colorado becomes the 38th state, and John Routt is elected its first state governor.

1877–John Routt buys the Morning Star Mine, a silver mine in Leadville, Colorado. Susan B. Anthony visits Colorado, but suffrage for women does not pass into law that fall, despite Governor Routt's support.

1879–John Routt strikes it rich with the Morning Star Mine, and starts living the life of a "Bonanza King." The Routts purchase a fine mansion at Fourteenth and Welton Streets in Denver. His first term as governor ends.

1880–A baby girl, Lila Elkin Routt, is born to John and Eliza Routt. Former President Grant visits the Routts and tours Colorado. Eliza's grandfather William Elkin, dies.

1882–The Routt's encourage the Reverend William Bayard Craig to come to Denver to take over the Central Christian Church, to which they donate large sums of money.

1883–John Routt is elected mayor of Denver for one term. He begins work on the board of Capitol Managers, serving until 1897.

1884–John Routt and sons buy ranch land near Fort Collins, Colorado.

1885–John Routt's term as mayor ends. He runs for the U.S. Senate and loses by four votes. Eliza's cousin Emma Pickrell marries Rev. William Bayard Craig. Grant dies.

1891–John Routt begins third term as governor. President Benjamin Harrison visits the Routts in Colorado.

1892–John Routt mediates the Creede Uprising.

1893–The silver market crashes when the Sherman Silver Mining Act is repealed, crushing Colorado's economy. Women's suffrage passes. Eliza Pickrell Routt is the first woman registered to vote in Colorado. John Routt's term as governor ends.

1894–The state capitol is completed at a cost of $2.8 million.

1895–Eliza Routt is elected to the Colorado State Board of Agriculture, where she is instrumental in the creation of a School of Domestic Economy.

1900–John, Eliza and Lila Routt travel to Europe. The Routt household in the Denver census lists John L., Eliza F., daughter Lila, son John A., and John's wife, Annie A.

1902–The Routts return to Denver and move into the Metropole Hotel. Lila makes her social debut.

1904–Eliza and Lila Routt become founding members of the Denver Chapter of the Daughters of the American Revolution.

1905–John Routt travels to Puerto Rico hoping the climate will improve his health. Eliza stays in Denver.

1906–Lila Routt marries Dr. Edward Welles Collins.

1907–Eliza Routt dies. John Routt dies less than five months later. They are buried in Riverside Cemetery in Denver.

1908–The state capitol's copper dome is replaced with a gold one.

1909–John Routt's stained glass window is installed in the Colorado State Capitol building. The Routt home at 1355 Welton is demolished.

Bibliography

Published Materials

Abbott, Carl, Stephen J. Leonard, and David McComb. *Colorado: A History of the Centennial State*. Niwot, Colo., University Press of Colorado, 1994.

Allers, W. W. and E. L. Gochanour. *History of Mechanicsburg Methodist Church*, Springfield, Ill.: n.p., 1986.

Arps, Louise Ward and Elinor Eppich Kingery. *High Country Names*, Estes Park, Colo: Rocky Mountain Nature Association, 1972.

Baggs, Mac Lacy. *Colorado: Crown Jewel of the Rockies*, Boston: The Page Company, 1918.

Baker, James H., ed., *History of Colorado*, Vol. 3, Denver: Linderman Company., Inc., 1927.

Bancroft, Caroline. *Augusta Tabor, Her Side of the Scandal*, Boulder, Colo.: Johnson Publishing Co., 1955.

__________. *Silver Queen, The Fabulous Story of Baby Doe Tabor*, Boulder, Colo.: Johnson Publishing Co., 1955.

Bateman, Newton and Paul Shelby, eds. *Historical Encyclopedia of Illinois and History of McLean County*, Vol. 2, Chicago: Munsell Publishing Company, 1908.

Bird, Isabella. *A Lady's Life in the Rocky Mountains*, 1879. Reprint, Sausalito, Calif.: Comstock Editions, Inc., 1987.

Blair, Edward. *Leadville: Colorado's Magic City*, Boulder, Colo.: Pruett Publishing Co., 1980.

Bueler, Gladys R. *Colorado's Colorful Characters*. Boulder, Colo.: Pruett Publishing Co., 1981.

Burke, John. *The Legend of Baby Doe*. Lincoln: University of Nebraska Press, 1974.

Byers, William N., *Encyclopedia of Biography of Colorado*, Vol. 1. Chicago: Century Publishing and Engraving Co., 1901.

Cannon, Helen. "First Ladies of Colorado—Eliza Pickrell Routt." *Colorado Magazine* 40, (January 1963): 48-56.

The Colorado Genealogist 19, no. 3, (July 1958).

Livestock Record, (February 1, 1884).

Constant, Rezin H., "Colorado as Seen by a Visitor of 1880." Diary. *Colorado Magazine*, 12, no. 3, (May 1935): 103-116.

Corbett, Thomas B., *Colorado Directory of Mines*, Denver: Rocky Mountain News Printing Co., 1879.

Corbett Hoye & Co., *Denver City Directories*. Rocky Mountain News Printing, 1880, p. 36; 1890, p. 1034; 1900, p. 1067; 1904, p. 1036 (microfilm, Denver Public Library).

Dorsett, Lyle W. *The Queen City: A History of Denver*. Boulder, Colo.: Pruett Publishing Co., 1977.

Duis, Dr. E., *The Good Old Times in McLean County, Illinois*. Bloomington, Ill: The Leader Publishing and Printing House, 1874.

Etheredge, Tracie L. *An Inventory of the Records of the Colorado Woman's Suffrage Association, Colorado State Equal Suffrage Association (1876-1881)*, Collection no. 1247. Denver: Colorado Historical Society, 1991.

Gilfillan, George and Ruth. "Among the Tailings, A Guide to Leadville Mines." *Herald Democrat*, (Leadville, Colo.), 1964.

Griswold, Don L., and Jean Harvey. *History of Leadville and Lake County, Colorado*, Denver: Colorado Historical Society in cooperation with the University Press of Colorado, 1996.

Hall, Frank. *History of the State of Colorado*. Chicago: The Blakely Printing Co., 1895.

Hansen, James E., II. *Democracy's College in the Centennial State, A History of Colorado State University*. Fort Collins, Colo.:Colorado State University, 1977.

Haynes, Nathaniel S. *History of the Disciples of Christ in Illinois 1819-1914*, Cincinnati, Ohio: Standard Publishing Co., 1915.

Inter-State Publishing Company. *History of Sangamon County, Illinois*. Chicago: Inter-State Publishing Co., 1881.

Iversen, Kristen. *Molly Brown: Unraveling the Myth*. Boulder, Colo.: Johnson Books, 1999.

Karsner, David, *Silver Dollar: The Story of the Tabors*. New York: Crown Publishers, 1932.

Lamm, Dottie. *Second Banana*. Boulder, Colo.: Johnson Books, 1983.

Lamm, Richard D. *Pioneers and Politicians*. Boulder, Colo.: Pruett Publishing Co., 1984.

Larimer County Stock Growers Association. *Larimer County Stock Growers Association Report*, Fort Collins, Colo. 1884-1956.

Leonard, Stephen J., and Thomas J. Noel. *Denver: Mining Camp to Metropolis*. Niwot, Colo.: University Press of Colorado, 1990.

Lisle, Merry Lynn. *John Long Routt Relationship List*. Denver: n.p., 1990.

Lorant, Stefan. *Lincoln*. New York: W.W. Norton and Co., Inc., 1969.

Miller, Francis Trevelyan, ed. *The Photographic History of the Civil War*, Vols. 1-20. New York: The Review of Reviews Co., 1912.

Moynihan, Betty. *Augusta Tabor, A Pioneering Woman*. Evergreen, Colo.: Cordillera Press Inc., 1988.

Noel, Thomas J. *Denver: Rocky Mountain Gold*. Tulsa, Okla.: Continental Heritage Press, 1980.

Pickrell Peers newsletters. Bakersfield, Calif., December 1979 and March 1981.
Pickrell, Mildred. *Descendants of Abel and Sarah (Taylor) Pickrell.* (family history, n.d.).
Porchea, Paul. *The Musical History of Colorado*. Denver: Charles Westley Publisher, 1889.
Portrait and Biographical Record of Denver and Vicinity, Colorado. Chicago: Chapman Publishing Co., 1898.
Power, John Carroll, *History of the Early Settlers of Sangamon County, Illinois*. Springfield, Ill.: Edwin A. Wilson & Co., 1876.
Russo, Edward J. *Prairie of Promise, Springfield and Sangamon County*. Woodland Hills, Calif.: Windsor Publications, 1983.
Sanford, Albert B. "John Routt, First State Governor of Colorado." *Colorado Magazine*. 3, no. 3, (August 1926): 81-87
Shelby, Paul, ed. *Historical Encyclopedia of Sangamon County*. Chicago: Munsell Publishing Co., 1912.
Simon, Dr. John Y., "Ulysses S. Grant," *World Book Encyclopedia 1999*. San Diego, Calif.: World Book Publishing, 1999.
Spilky, Scott. "Learning about Lincoln at the University of Illinois." *Illinois Alumni*, 12, no. 2, (September/October 1999): 18-23.
Sons of Colorado, 1, no. 11, (April 1907):22.
Teetor, Henry Dudley. "Hon. John L. Routt, Ex-Governor of Colorado." *Magazine of Western History*, 9, no. 4, (February 1889): 457-460.
Turner, Wallace B. *Colorado Woman's College: the Story of a Dream*. Marceline, Mo.:Walsworth Publishing Company, 1982.
Ubbelohde, Carl, Maxine Benson, and Duane A. Smith. *A Colorado History*. Boulder, Colo.: Pruett Publishing Co., 1995.
Voight, Robert Charles. *The Life of John Long Routt*. Master's thesis.Colorado State College of Education (Greeley, Colo.), 1947.
Voynick, Stephen M. *Leadville: A Miner's Epic*. Missoula, Mont.,: Mountain Press Publishing Co., 1984.
Walkup, Janna C. *The Victorian Lady*. Eugene, Ore.: Harvest House Publishers, 1998.
Wallace, Joseph. *Past and Present of the City of Springfield and Sangamon County, Illinois*. Vol. 2, Chicago: The S.J. Clarke Publishing Company, 1904.

Web Sites

"Colorado State Capitol Virtual Tour," Colorado State Archives, http://www.archives.state.co.us/cap/gold.htm
Descendants of John Constant, Elkin/Constant genealogy, http://www.parsonstech.com/genealogy/trees/dlund123/constant.htm
Dyer, Frederick H., "History of the Illinois 94th Infantry." In *A Compendium of the War of the Rebellion*, Des Moines, Iowa: The Dyer Publishing Co., 1908. http://www.rootsweb.com/~ilcivilw/dyers/094inf.htm.
"John Long Routt," Colorado State Archives, http://www.state.co.us/gov_dir/gss/archives/govs/routt.html

Thompson, Leonard G., "William Byrd [*sic*] Craig." In *Churches of Christ*, edited by John T. Brown, 1904.
http://www.mun.ca/rels/restmov/texts/jtbrown/coc/COC1357.htm

Libraries and Archives

Colorado Historical Society, Stephen H. Hart Library, Denver, Colorado
Colorado State Archives, Denver, Colorado
Colorado State University Archives, Fort Collins, Colorado
Denver Public Library, Western History Department, Denver, Colorado
Fort Collins Public Library, Fort Collins, Colorado
Lake County Courthouse, Leadville, Colorado
Larimer County Courthouse, Fort Collins, Colorado
Norlin Library, University of Colorado, Boulder, Colorado
Riverside and Fairmount Cemeteries, Denver, Colorado
Ulysses S. Grant Association, Carbondale, Illinois
United States National Archives, Washington, D.C.

Correspondence

Nobles, Lila. Telephone conversations, written correspondence with author, March 2000.

O'Connell, Dorothy. Telephone conversations, written correspondence with author, February 1999.

Newspapers

Daily News/Rocky Mountain News, Denver, Colorado
Daily Republican, Decatur, Illinois
Denver Post, Denver, Colorado
Denver Republican, Denver, Colorado
Denver Times, Denver, Colorado
Denver Weekly Mirror, Denver, Colorado
Fort Collins Courier, Fort Collins, Colorado
Fort Collins Weekly Express, Fort Collins, Colorado
Great Divide, Denver, Colorado
Harper's Weekly
Queen Bee, Denver, Colorado

Documents

Death certificates for John L. Routt, Eliza P. Routt, and Lila Routt Bryant, Denver City-County Building, Vital Records Office, Denver, Colo.

Deeds for ranchland purchased by John L. Routt and sons, 1884-1885, (Grantee) Index Book #3, recorded in Books 34, 38, and 44, Larimer County Courthouse.

Guardianship Record, children of Benjamin F. Pickrell, June 11, 1840, Illinois State Regional Archives, Springfield, Ill., Guardian's Case File Index 1825-1902, Case #199.

Hotel Rate Ads, Brown Palace and Metropole Hotel, September 1892, courtesy of Brown Palace Hotel, Denver, Colo.

Illinois Public Domain Land Tract Sales Database, vol. 068, pp. 121 and 164, Illinois Regional Archives, Springfield, Ill.

Interment and Daily Activity Records for Fairmount and Riverside Cemeteries, 1907, Fairmount Cemetery Company, Denver, Colo.

Invitation for the International Exhibition of 1877, to His Excellency John L. Routt and Lady, Philadelphia, April 2, 1877, #9353, Colorado State Archives.

Invitation for the International Mining and Industrial Exposition to Hon. John L. Routt, March 8, 1895, Denver, Colo., #9353, Colorado State Archives.

Invitation for World's Columbian Exposition to Hon. John L. Routt, October 19, 1893, #9353, Colorado State Archives.

Larimer County Ranch Map and Appointment of Larimer County Associate Supreme Court Justice, signed by John L. Routt, September 1876, Fort Collins Public Library.

Leadville Mine Maps, ca. 1880, Western History Department, Denver Public Library.

Letter from President Benjamin Harrison to Hon. John L. Routt, June 14, 1892, #9353, Colorado State Archives.

Letter from A. Lincoln to Jesse A. Pickrell, Nov. 3, 1859, Springfield, Ill., author's copy.

Letters from John L. Routt to Eliza F. Pickrell, March 5, 1874—June 4, 1874, #9353, Colorado State Archives.

Letter from John L. Routt, 1876, published by Cyril Clemens, from Denver Public Library, Western History Department.

Letter from Attorney Charles A. Stokes to Mrs. Eliza F. Routt, March 11, 1905, #9353, Colorado State Archives.

Marriage Notice from *Decatur (Illinois) Republican* for Eliza Pickrell and John Routt, MSS #977, Stephen H. Hart Library, Colorado Historical Society.

Marriage License, John L. Routt and Eliza F. Pickrell, May 21, 1874, Macon County (Illinois) County Clerk and Recorder.

Obituary for William F. Elkin, MSS #977, Stephen H. Hart Library, Colorado Historical Society,

Quit-Claim Deed for Morning Star Mine, October 22, 1877, Book C, Page 227, Lake County Courthouse.

Receipt of Gov. J.L. Routt amount subscribed in order to defray expenses to Gen. Grant's funeral, July 28, 1885, #9353, Colorado State Archives.

State Board of Agriculture Minutes, Book #2, Dec. 8, 1886 through April 25, 1905, Colorado State University Archives.

Telegram to Gov. John L. Routt with invitation from President Harrison, Clear Creek, Colo., May 9, 1891, #9353, Colorado State Archives.

United States Census, Arapahoe County, Colo., 1880, p. 126; 1885, pp. 9, 46; 1900, p.52.

United States Census, McLean County, Ill., 1850, p. 14.

United States Census, Macon County, Ill., 1870, p. 379.

United States Census, Sangamon County, Ill., 1850, p. 290; 1860, pp. 113, 349.
United States Marshal Appointment, John L. Routt, signed by Ulysses S. Grant, March 2, 1870, #9353, Colorado State Archives.
United States National Archives, Washington, D.C., Civil War Records for John L. Routt, 94th Illinois Infantry, Company E, Union Army.
United States National Archives, War of 1812, Abel Pickrel's Muster Record, Johnson's Mounted Regiment, #1617.

Index

About the Author

Photographer: Don Lohse

JOYCE BURKE LOHSE, lives in Centennial, Colorado, with her husband, Don, and their son, Charlie. She grew up in Illinois and holds a journalism degree from Northern Illinois University. Joyce serves on the board of directors for the Columbine Genealogical and Historical Society, and on the board of Women Writing the West. She has been a volunteer and docent at the Colorado Historical Society. Joyce's previous publications include *A Yellowstone Savage: Life in Nature's Wonderland*, an insider's view of living and working in Yellowstone National Park, and numerous magazine articles. Her passion for genealogy research led her to the fascinating story of her ancestral cousin, Eliza Pickrell Routt.